# THE SEARCH FOR THE REAL JESUS

# THE SEARCH FOR THE REAL JESUS

## DAVID WINTER

**MOREHOUSE-BARLOW CO., INC.**
**Wilton, Connecticut**

The Scripture quotations in this book are generally taken from the New International Version, published by Hodder & Stoughton.

ISBN 0-8192-1318-7

First U.S. edition, 1982
Morehouse-Barlow Co., Inc.
78 Danbury Road
Wilton, Connecticut 06897

*Printed in the United States of America*

# CONTENTS

# INTRODUCTION

I have called this book 'The Search for the Real Jesus'. That implies that the 'real' Jesus has to be looked for, and also, I suppose, that there is the possibility of people discovering a bogus or unreal Jesus. I think both implications have some truth in them. If they do not, then this book would represent a rather pointless exercise.

Some people may be surprised at the suggestion that there is any need to 'search' for Jesus. Surely, they will say, he is there in the pages of the Gospels? Most people in the Western world are familiar with the story of his life, even if only in a fragmentary way. They know about his birth at Bethlehem, about the shepherds and the Wise Men and the young virgin mother, Mary. They know some of his parables, if only from phrases that have entered into most of our languages: the seed that falls on stony soil, the mote in the eye, the Good Samaritan. And they know of his death on a cross, commemorated in hundreds of millions of replicas in wood, silver or gold strung around a similar number of necks. So, what is there to 'search' for? Is not the very suggestion an unnecessary complication of what we have come to call 'Gospel truth'?

But the issue is not as simple as that, as an increasing number of people are coming to find. A plethora of books over recent decades, since Albert Schweitzer's *The Quest for the Historical Jesus*, have made them aware that nearly two thousand years of intervening history, vast changes in culture and lifestyle, and new understandings of ancient literature have raised questions where once all was certainty and assurance. Several of the more recent books have been picked up and quoted in the press, on television and radio, and have given many people the idea that the Gospels are totally unreliable as historical documents. The word 'myth' has been bandied about freely. Perhaps, it is suggested, somewhere behind the mists of legend and the distortions of centuries of credulous piety, there *was* a person called Jesus. Perhaps he said and did some of the things that are related in the Gospels and believed − offici- ally − by Christians. Perhaps something of his 'spirit' remains to inspire men and women today. *Perhaps*. The message that has got through to many people − rightly or wrongly − is that Jesus of Nazareth no longer has historical credibility and that therefore the cutting edge of Christian- ity is blunted. Shorn of its base in history, it becomes merely one of many competing philosophies and 'life stances', to be accepted or rejected on the basis of what suits the believer rather than what is true.

So, the 'search' is important. For a religion as rooted in history as Christianity, there is no evading it. If Jesus did not live, or did not say and do what Christians believe he said and did, then it is hard to see how it can survive. It is not, like Hinduism, a kind of 'feeling', nor, like Buddhism, a perspective on reality. It is, as its proponents have often argued, 'Jesus Christ, crucified and risen'. After all, it was Christianity's first great advocate, St Paul, who said, 'If Christ is not risen, then our faith is in vain'. Everything stands or falls on Jesus, and if we cannot in any sense rely on the records we have of him, then the world's greatest religion loses its most distinctive feature, and the history of the human race its most attractive personality.

The search has been going on for a long while, of course. For the most part it has been confined to fairly heavyweight academic books and articles in specialist journals, though recently the general public has caught whiffs of it in the Sunday colour supplements and on the TV screen. At one point it seemed that the scholars had given up in despair, and were on the verge of saying that it was impossible to rediscover the Jesus of history.

But the last decade has seen an amazing transformation. Now, the Jesus of history seems more accessible than ever. Like archaeologists swarming over a prime location, the historians and theologians have turned with gusto to the original documents, parallel historical records and the geographical sites, and at every turn have found a clearer and clearer picture emerging of Jesus of Nazareth.

Not all of them are agreed about the details of that picture, of course. But there is a growing consensus about its main features, and it is with them that this book is concerned. Any sensible search begins with what is known and then proceeds step by step from there into the less charted areas. So this search for Jesus begins with the consensus — what is common to all but the most idiosyncratic scholars — and then tries to build a fuller picture piece by piece on that foundation.

It is perhaps a little pretentious to claim that what we are in search of is the 'real' Jesus, with the obvious implication that other people's searches have led them to the wrong person. But it does seem to me to be obvious that some of the pictures of Jesus which we have been offered in recent years — and some of the pictures offered to people in past centuries, too – bear only a passing resemblance to the Jesus of the Gospels. The Middle Ages gave us Christ the King, sitting on his remote throne and judging the nations of mankind with an iron rod. The Pietists gave us Jesus the heavenly Lover. The Victorians gave us the manly Christ, the straight-eyed, fair-faced young athlete of the illustrated Bibles. In our day we have added many more Christs: the liberal Jesus, who is found in nature, beauty and love, an endless incarnation of kindness and good taste; the political Jesus, who endorses whatever is the current protest or panacea; and Christ the Liberator, a kind of first-century Che Guevara. All have been preached and followed, and all reflect something of the 'original'. But none does him justice.

To say that one is setting out to search for the real Jesus is not to claim that one has found him. Quite the contrary. It is an admission that somewhere along the line we have lost him, and need to re-focus our lenses, remove the dust of centuries and the preconceptions of the present, and look for him afresh. Nor is it to imply that nobody else has ever found him, or is finding him today. Manifestly, that would be nonsense. One of the reasons for the current fascination with the subject of Jesus is that so many people across the world are coming to faith in him, and the enthusiasm of these disciples is infectious. But such a degree of interest makes it more important, not less, that the picture we have of him is as accurate as we can get it. If he is a person of history, and if he founded a great religion, we are not free to re-draw him or re-write it to suit our twentieth-century needs. We are shut in to the Jesus who existed. If we wish to start a new religion, let us give it some other name than Christianity.

So it is important for the believer to join in this search. It is not a denial of what he believes already. It is not a contradiction of faith in someone to want to know them better. Not only that, but many Christians are baffled and worried by things they have heard or read about Jesus – things which seem to contradict their own 'faith-experience' of him. They want to believe in the 'real' Jesus: who prefers substitutes? For them, the Jesus of history is the only valid and reliable basis for the Jesus of their faith.

There are also, of course, many unbelievers who are attracted to Jesus, but are not sure whether the picture of him which is offered to them is really credible. They, too, may be aware of the scholarly debate about the Gospels. They may find the miraculous element difficult, or the resurrection, or (most often) the Christian belief that Jesus of Nazareth was, and is, the Son of God. For them, the question 'How should we see Jesus?' needs to be answered before they can be expected to answer the more decisive question, 'Will you put your faith in him?'

This book, then, is for people – believers or unbelievers – who want to know about Jesus, and are prepared to put into that search some time and some serious thought. The method is to start from the consensus that I mentioned, the outline of the life of Jesus that is broadly accepted as historical, and then to build from that, as carefully as possible, until the picture is as full as we can make it without either wild speculation or the exercise of faith. Then, and only then, we move on to the Jesus of faith – the Jesus whom Christians believe in and the Church preaches – to see if and how far this is a reasonable extension of the Jesus of history. Of course, historical methods and painstaking research cannot bring a person to a living faith in Jesus Christ. But I believe that they are the only reasonable basis for that faith, and for many people anything less leaves them with a literally incredible Jesus.

Some readers may not unreasonably ask why this particular search is more likely to bring them to the 'real' Jesus than all the others. It cannot be claimed, I admit, that there has been any shortage of books on the subject in recent years. Some have been much more sceptical than this one; some have been much more conservative. What I would claim is that few have started from the same point as this one and yet ended where this one does.

I am not a scholar, but a layman who has spent his working life in teaching, journalism and, now, broadcasting, trying to communicate Christian faith to modern people. More and more I have become aware of a credibility gap between the Church's statements of faith and ordinary men and women's threshold of belief. People would like to believe, and want to believe, but they find a yawning gulf between the ordinary twentieth-century world in which they live and the world of the Bible. Some make the leap of faith, and reach the other side. Some make the leap, but fall short and retire hurt. Many, however, simply stand on the brink helplessly, or else walk away. I want to start on their side, and end up with them on the other.

I am not, myself, a 'natural' believer − the sort of person to whom faith comes easily. I am cursed with the journalist's disease, cynicism. I do not take easily to the world of the supernatural or mystical. Nevertheless, I have found the experience of working on this book profoundly positive. As I have pored over the books and documents, and talked with scholars in Britain and in Israel, layers of misunderstanding, preconceptions and cultural conditioning have been removed from my eyes. My faith in the Jesus of the Gospels − an obstinately orthodox one, I might add − has been strengthened, or perhaps, more honestly, transformed.

I guess that many people – Christians and sympathetic enquirers – are ready to share my experience, not because I am the most authoritative guide, but because the *method* appeals to them. It may seem a strange one to some believers, because the book does not start with an assumption that the Bible is an inspired authority on the subject of Jesus. But this is to be no more than realistic. The reason people do not believe that Jesus is the Son of God is that they do not accept the inspired authority of the Bible. Obviously if they did they would have no choice but to accept its witness to the divinity of Jesus. So, for many interested, sympathetic but as yet unconvinced people, books about Jesus which assume that authority are inadequate – and there are plenty of books which do. It is not much use telling someone whose main doubts about Jesus concern the reliability of the evidence about him that 'the Bible' says this or 'the Gospels' say that, as though that clinched the argument.

So this particular search tries to take as little for granted as possible. That is why the first four chapters are concerned with the sources of the evidence about Jesus, and their value as a basis for discovering the Jesus of history. Readers who have no problems about the reliability of the Gospels can, if they prefer, start at Chapter 5, and go back to the opening section if they find that the reconstruction of the life of Jesus offered in the second half of the book raises doubts about the historical methods used or the evidence on which the book is built.

# 1

## THE JESUS OF HISTORY?

In AD 29, by the River Jordan in the Roman province of Peraea, a man appeared on the public scene who was to have a greater influence on the subsequent history of the world than anyone who has ever lived, before or since. His first public act was to be baptised in the River Jordan; his last – it is claimed – was to rise from the dead. In the nineteen hundred years since those events, the religion which he founded has become the largest and most influential in human history, and today a third of the world's population believe that he is the Son of God.

Jesus simply cannot be ignored. As a figure of history, as a moulder of human thoughts and attitudes and as an example of ideal humanity, he has won the admiration and devotion of many of the world's greatest men and women. Belief in him has survived the superstition and ignorance of the Dark Ages, the scepticism of the modern world and persecution by his outraged rivals. It has also survived, though more narrowly, the clumsy efforts of organised Christianity to fit him into various man-made power structures.

I have said that Jesus cannot be ignored, but that is only half the truth. The fact is that many modern people, even in the supposedly 'Christian' part of the world, *do* ignore him, apparently as a deliberate policy. But even more people, generally through no fault of their own, have access only to a distorted picture of him, and reject not Jesus as he was (and is, to faith), but as he has been presented to them. They have various scraps and pieces of information about him, a few parables and miracles, the birth stories which are part of the Christmas mystique, and the image of a body nailed to a cross. They have probably never read any of the four Gospels, which are the primary sources by which we know about him; at any rate, not right through, nor consecutively. And even if they are fairly regular church-goers, all that that will have added to their knowledge of Jesus is probably the fact that his mother was Mary, and that he instituted a ritual meal in his own memory, which is universally celebrated to this day, and in which bread and wine are said to become, or represent (according to various traditions) his body and blood.

So in practice there is a great ignorance about Jesus, even among Christians. Few people have much idea how they should approach the Gospels, and few preachers, to be honest, give them much help. Every now and then a tiny puff of information leaks from the enclaves of the scholars and causes panic amongst the faithful, for all the world like a leak from a defective nuclear power station. But the security forces of the Church move in quickly to repair the damage, and it is soon forgotten by most people. Such books as *Honest to God*[1], *The Myth of God Incarnate*[2], *Taking Leave of God*[3] and *Jesus: An Experiment in Christology*[4], seized on briefly and presented sensationally by the press, have caused such moments of disquiet, but few ordinary Christians have had their view of Jesus permanently changed by them.

The position of the unbeliever, especially the sympathetic unbeliever, is rather different. His difficulties about Jesus are not concerned with preserving the status quo, but with coming to terms with an attractive but elusive historical figure. If he turns to the Gospels, he finds himself in an unfamiliar literary *genre*, in which the person of Jesus as teacher and prophet may seem to him at odds with the 'other' Jesus, who works amazing miracles and is regarded, and appears to regard himself, as the Son of God. If he goes to church and listens to sermons, he finds exactly the same tension. Some preach Jesus as though he were a modern radical reformer, a prophet for every age. Others proclaim an other-worldly Jesus, an incarnation (no less) of God himself, who is alive and active in human affairs and is still working his miracles in the lives of believers.

Most common of all, however, is the 'Project Jesus', which is little more than the characterisation of an ideal.

Somewhere down inside most human beings is the notion of the 'ideal person', representing all the things we most admire and would most like to be – gentle yet strong, just but fair, wise yet humble. It is a tiny step to give that ideal a name and call it 'Jesus', projecting on to him, as an object of admiration and even veneration, our notion of a perfected humanity.

Now there is more than an element of truth in each of these portraits, but none of them starts at the right place (who is Jesus?) and consequently none does justice to the real Jesus, who is not the creation of our ideas, or a projection of our ideals, but a man of history.

If the searcher goes so far as to buy one of the scores of scholarly books about Jesus that have been published in the last few years, he will encounter a further set of problems. Here he will find himself in a new dilemma. He will probably feel like somebody who has taken his seat in a cinema halfway through an exciting but complicated film. All of the books are enthusiastic about their subject, the authors are clearly fascinated by Jesus and determined to reinstate him as an important and decisive figure in human history.

But for the most part they pre-suppose the reader's familiarity with the plot thus far. Unfamiliar names and concepts abound – Bultmann, form criticism, 'Q', demythologisation, the synoptic problem – which are clearly the everyday concern of the author and his intended readership. So the interested unbeliever gives up the search for Jesus in despair, just as many believers have abandoned any attempt seriously to come to grips with the Jesus of history, the *real* Jesus who lived and taught and died and, they believe, rose again in Palestine nearly two thousand years ago.

Yet Jesus *can* be known. We live in a privileged age, when the labours of great theological scholars and the discoveries of archaeologists and historians have made it possible, as never before, to read the New Testament with real perception, and to piece together from it, and other sources, a true and wholly convincing portrait of Jesus. But many Christians are afraid of biblical scholarship, fearful that it exists to undermine and eventually to destroy faith. Alec Vidler, in the preface to his excellent paperback on Mark's Gospel[5], quotes with approval some words of a reviewer in *Theology* about biblical scholars who write books aimed at the ordinary reader:

> They obviously realize to how great an extent the 'person in the pew' can conceive of nothing other than a literalist interpretation of the Bible, but feels unhappy with it, whereas no other approach to the Bible has ever been adequately, if at all, represented to him. As a result he rarely reads his Bible. Many 'popular' books on the Bible and its use seem . . . to be written out of the conviction that it is actually undesirable to present the methods and achievements of New Testament scholarship to any interested layman, because this scholarship is assumed by their authors to be hostile to such a person's faith.

In fact, the scholars are in a position to provide the clues we must have if our understanding of Jesus is to be genuinely biblical, and not simply the projection of our own needs. Without help, few people can possibly hope to interpret the Gospels (or the letters of Paul, for that matter) as the original authors intended. What they will tend to do is to find in the biblical material a verse here, or a saying there, or a miracle or a parable, that meets an immediate need, and clutch it to themselves. Eventually they may well construct a substantial image of Jesus from such material, but it may not be the biblical Jesus at all.

I have heard many a statement in Bible study groups, or in conversation with devout Christians, that has betrayed their belief in a Jesus who is simply *not* the one the Gospels describe, or the apostles believed in. Thus many Christians, including many who would claim to believe the Bible totally and even literally, *in practice* are existentialists. They have made a Jesus to suit their needs, but he is not the one who lived in Palestine and died on a cross. Though they may deeply resent it, they need the help of the scholars — 'discriminatingly received', as Alec Vidler puts it — to correct their vision of Jesus.

But the searcher − the interested unbeliever − also needs their help. Before rejecting the Gospels as hopelessly infiltrated by myth and legend, or deciding that it is impossible to know anything with certainty about this man of history, he might agree that it is right to make time to ensure that he has not pre-judged one of the most important decisions of any human being's life: how do I respond to Jesus?

It will take time, because the Gospels are complex, demanding books. Morna Hooker, Lady Margaret Professor of Divinity at Cambridge, has said:

There is no such thing as 'pure history' in the New Testament (nor indeed anywhere else). The documents we have were all written by committed men from a standpoint of faith. They are in fact propaganda. We cannot distil the historical facts out of the accounts; the interpretation has been built into the material by men who believed in Jesus.

Our scientific colleagues tell me that if iron and sulphur are mixed together it is a comparatively easy process to separate them again with a magnet. But once they have been fused into iron sulphide, they are inseparable. In the Gospels, historical accounts and interpretation have been fused together in the accounts with which the evangelists present us.[6]

But the difficulty for the searcher coming to this material does not end with this confusion of history and interpretation. The 'message' about Christ is expressed in the Gospels in terms of first-century culture. Phrases like 'Son of Man', 'Son of God', 'the Word', 'Messiah' and 'the kingdom of heaven' may *seem* familiar to us, and even easy to understand. In fact, they may present severe hazards for the unwary modern reader.

Yet that 'message' − the message about Jesus − is vital. The men and women of this generation need it every bit as much as did the people of the first century. We, too, long for understanding, for acceptance with God, for forgiveness, for meaning and purpose; and we, too, sense that they may be found in the towering figure of Jesus.

This book is an attempt to pursue that search, gratefully and discriminatingly using the work of biblical and other scholars, in the hope that at the end the believer may find his faith enriched, and the searcher find not the Jesus of fable or fantasy, but the Jesus of history.

# 2
# WHAT IS THE EVIDENCE?

Jesus lived two thousand years ago, in an obscure corner of the Roman Empire. All the contemporary records of what he said and did do not amount to more than a slim paperback book. The great secular historians of the period, including the leading chronicler of Jewish history, Josephus, do not give him much more than a passing mention. And yet, as we have seen, the faith of a thousand million people in the twentieth century depends on that slender evidence.

It is as though in the twentieth century a philosopher had lived and taught and died in, say, Madagascar, without evoking more than a passing reference in the newspapers and magazines of the civilised world and totally ignored by the international academic establishment. His 'career' lasted no more than three years, and yet within twenty years of his death an enormous cult developed far beyond his native land. His collected sayings, recalled or recorded by those who had known him, became the subject of worldwide analysis and study. Any reminiscence, however trivial, was avidly seized upon; and, of course, there was no shortage of spurious 'recollections' by those anxious to jump on the band-waggon. Eventually the cultural establishment, without much enthusiasm, was forced to admit that the philosopher from Madagascar had been an important and formative figure.

Even though we push the scene back twenty centuries, to the time of Jesus, it is stupid to claim in circumstances like these that nothing can be known for certain about the man, simply because there was a time-lag between his words and actions ('the event') and their committal to writing ('the record'). Such a time-lag is a common-place of history until modern times, and still is, in the kind of example we have just considered. Equally, however, it would be unrealistic to deny that this whole process does create problems for anyone who wants to know, with certainty, what was said and what was done.

In the case of Jesus, all we have to go on is what some of his contemporaries recalled. That recollection is necessarily influenced by their later conviction that he was the Messiah, because the only detailed record we have is by his own followers. This is hardly surprising in the circumstances — Jesus simply did not seem 'important' enough to the intellectuals of his day, which only serves to show how wrong intellectuals can be.

So there are obvious difficulties in establishing in a scientific way the facts about Jesus, but they are by no means insuperable.

For a hundred years, at least, scholars have worked at the New Testament texts, and the secular history of the period, in an attempt to reconstruct 'the historical Jesus'. More recently, some have rejected this search, believing that it is in fact impossible, an illusion. That was the view of the German theologian, Rudolf Bultmann. But, according to Professor Morna Hooker, they have given up too easily — or set themselves unreasonably demanding goals:

Many New Testament scholars are notoriously sceptical and seem to colleagues in the fields of ancient and later history to demand far more evidence than can reasonably be expected. Evidence for historical occurrences can never, in fact, be one hundred per cent certain; there is always room for ifs and buts. Most historians do not expect more than a balance of probabilities. Possibly as the result of an inbuilt pressure, a desire to be objective and not to claim too much in a field where he might be thought to be biased, the Christian New Testament scholar is often unduly sceptical, and falls over backwards in an attempt to be objective. In the process, he may well get the wrong historical answer. Certainly he often shows an amazing imagination in suggesting alternative explanations.[1]

In fact, today most biblical scholars *do* believe that it is possible to establish a reliable historical basis for the life of Jesus, and that over and beyond that a reasonably full picture of him can be reconstructed from the Gospels. Their work may seem unduly sceptical to the believer, and the kernel which they are prepared to accept as undoubtedly historical too small. But for the interested unbeliever, this may well seem the most promising way to approach Jesus: to start with what is demonstrably true, and then to build on that from the Gospel records, piece by piece, until he has a convincing picture of Jesus. This in turn can become the base for a genuine act of faith – not an irrational acceptance of the unlikely, but a commitment to what is both reasonable and demanding.

The process by which scholars have sought to reconstruct a picture of Jesus the man is a fascinating one, and it is a valuable exercise to see how they go about it.

It is, as one might expect, a formidably difficult undertaking. James P. Mackey – admittedly a sceptic among New Testament scholars – has set out a list of the difficulties where the sources of reliable information about Jesus are concerned:

That Jesus himself left no written records; that the earliest written record of the movement he started comes from the pen of a man, Paul, who to the best of our knowledge never met him in the flesh, and who begins to write about him some twenty years after his death; that the only writings, the gospels as they are called, which purport to give any substantial information about his life, are written from about AD 70, about forty years after his death, to the nineties of the first century . . . that apart from the writings of the New Testament, which range in date from about AD 50 to well into the second century, and which are all written by convinced followers of Jesus to persuade others to follow him, only the barest references to his existence can be gleaned from other writings of the time.[2]

One need not accept all Mackey's judgements – I do not, as we shall see – to accept that there *are* huge difficulties to face.

So how, in view of such problems, does the scholar set about his search for the 'Jesus of history'? His first step is usually to establish the environment, the setting in which Jesus appeared. A good deal is known about the Roman Empire of this period, and contemporary documents, Roman and Jewish, vividly re-create a period of political and religious crisis in Palestine. Warring religious factions, as we shall see later in more detail, were united only in their detestation of the hated oppressors, the Romans. Riots and retaliatory massacres were common. Political saviours appeared on the scene with daunting regularity, only to disappear as swiftly as they had appeared. It was a period of change, of turmoil and of widespread expectation on the part of the Jews: surely God would soon intervene?

Into this environment, and identified with one of the leading religious revival movements of the day, led by John the Baptiser, came Jesus. His connection with John, and the dating of John's strange revivalist movement, are both well established – they met in the fifteenth year of the reign of Tiberius, AD 29.

The next definite fixed point in the life of Jesus is in fact his death, by crucifixion, during the proconsulship of Pontius Pilate. It is well attested both by the Gospel writers and by secular history, and the known dates of Pilate fix it between AD 30 and AD 36 – probably AD 32.

That is more or less the sum total of what one might call verifiable historical fact about Jesus; but the experts are fairly certain about the main content of his teaching, too. As we shall see, such concepts as the 'kingdom of God' (understood very differently from others who had used the term), the fatherhood of God (in a more intimate way than his contemporaries saw it), the universality of the love of God and the institution of a fellowship meal are generally recognised as distinctive to Jesus.

James P. Mackey summarises the position about the teaching of Jesus – his 'cause', as he puts it – in these words:

We shall be on ground as solid as the best scholarly research can provide if, in searching for the cause of Jesus for which he lived and died, in searching for the only life of Jesus that mattered to him or to us, we look for the meaning that he gave to that phrase 'the Kingdom of God' in his parables, his prayer, and his practical ministry of 'miracle' and meal.[3]

We shall look at those inverted commas around the word 'miracle' later, but Mackey concedes strong historical evidence here, too:

> The memory that some extraordinary healings . . . occurred during the ministry of Jesus is so embedded in all strata of the early tradition, and even in some references to Jesus in Jewish literature, as to give the highest likelihood of the historicity of some such events.[4]

The next stage in the reconstruction of the Jesus of the historians (rather, perhaps, than the Jesus of history) is to consider the widely-held belief of his first followers that he had risen from the dead. The earliest account we have of the life of Jesus is the brief summary given by St Paul at the end of his first letter to the Corinthians. It was written about AD 55, and pre-dates the earliest Gospel, Mark, by several years:

> I passed on to you first of all the message I had myself received − that Christ died for our sins, as the scriptures said he would; that he was buried and rose again on the third day, as the scriptures foretold. He was seen by Cephas (Peter), then by the twelve, and subsequently he was seen simultaneously by over five hundred Christians, of whom the majority are still alive, though some have since died. He was then seen by James, then by all the messengers.[5]

Now there is no doubt about the historicity of Paul, very little, if any, about the authenticity of this letter, and not much argument about its date. He is quoting, he says, from a tradition that was handed on to him after his conversion in the early years of the Church. So it is interesting that he should give as the central beliefs of that infant Christian Church the death of Jesus 'for our sins' and his resurrection from the dead, and that he should base his argument for the latter not primarily on his own mystical experience or vision of Jesus on the Damascus road, but on the existence of eye-witnesses of the resurrection, 'the majority of whom are still alive'.

Paul was writing just over twenty years after the crucifixion, so it was indeed likely that most of those who had seen the risen Jesus, who were mostly young men and women at the time, would still be alive. It was their testimony which could be checked and cross-examined. It is certainly the claim of a man who is confident of his facts

Obviously we cannot put the resurrection of Jesus into the category of things that are historically provable. But it *is* an historical fact that the early Christians believed it. Vast numbers of Christians in the first century — hundreds of thousands, very probably — believed that Jesus, executed in Jerusalem in AD 32, rose from the dead. And they believed this, and publicly asserted it against all opposition, well within the lifetime of the eye-witnesses of the crucifixion. As we shall see, that in itself is a very important piece of evidence relating to Jesus.

So the skeleton on which our portrait of Jesus is based grows more complete. We have the appearance of Jesus associated with John the Baptiser, his typical and possibly unique teaching and healing ministry, his death by crucifixion, and the widespread belief of his followers that he rose from the dead. We can place these events within fairly precise dates and relate all of them to other, known historical characters and events.

But anyone familiar with the Gospels will see at once that two substantial elements of the life of Jesus, as most people have understood it from the New Testament, fall outside this historical skeleton. The first concerns the miracles which Jesus is described as performing; the second concerns his birth and the narratives in the first and third Gospels about it.

We shall be looking at these in more detail later, but for now it has to be conceded that they cannot, for different reasons, be regarded as part of that historically verifiable core of the life of Jesus. That does not mean that they did not happen, nor even that they are intrinsically incredible or even unlikely. But it is virtually impossible to *prove* a miracle after the event, and the birth narratives, which are not mentioned in the earliest records of Jesus, pose particular problems for the historian.

However, where the miracles are concerned there is a similar point to make as was made concerning the resurrection. Although one cannot prove that Jesus did miracles, it is (as we have already mentioned) part of the historical record that he was widely known as a miracle-worker, both by his friends and his enemies. In other words, contemporary records (not subsequent embellishment) speak of Jesus as a teacher who also healed and carried out exorcisms.

With regard to the birth narratives, two details *can* be regarded as historically verifiable. There is irresistible testimony to the fact that Jesus was 'from Nazareth', and there seems no reason at all to doubt that his mother's name was Mary and his father's Joseph. By nothing more complicated than simple subtraction we can arrive at the date of birth for Jesus in the two to five years before what we now (erroneously) know as AD 1.

So we have the 'outline' of the life of Jesus. He was born in, say, 2 BC. His parents were called Joseph and Mary, and he grew up in Nazareth. At about the age of thirty (probably rather older) he emerged as a teacher and miracle-worker, associated at first with the movement of religious reform led by John the Baptiser in Galilee. He proclaimed, however, a distinctive set of beliefs and gained a considerable reputation as a healer and exorcist. In (about) AD 32 he was crucified under the jurisdiction of Pontius Pilate, and within a short time his followers were claiming that he had risen from the dead.

Finally, as a kind of postscript, we can say that by AD 70

the Christian religion was established virtually throughout the Roman Empire. It was growing rapidly, despite constant, and at times vicious, opposition by the authorities, Jewish, Greek or Roman. And its message – what we now have in the first three Gospels and the first nine epistles attributed to St Paul[6] – was that Jesus of Nazareth, the Jesus of history, the self-styled 'Son of Man', was none other than the Son of God.

# 3

# THE FIRST RECORD: MARK

It is early evening in Rome sometime during AD 60. In the cellars of the splendid home of a city gentleman a group of people is gathering. They arrive in twos and threes, hurrying along the dark street outside and climbing down a flight of steps to the cellar door, where they rap a signal and are admitted by a tall, dark man in the tunic of a slave.

Once inside, however, the air of furtive anxiety disappears. Newcomers are greeted with warmth and there is plenty of laughter and animated conversation. A single oil lamp flickers on a central table, emphasising the darkness of the deeper recesses of the room, and casting moving shadows on the stone ceiling, the solid pillars that hold it up and the faces of the people.

The make-up of the gathering would baffle an outsider. Uniquely, for ancient Rome, those present are more or less a cross-section of the sort of people to be seen in a city street: men and women, young and old, patricians and plebs, freemen, foreigners and slaves. Yet they seem to observe no social barriers. A slave talks to a merchant; a young woman in plebeian clothes talks to an older woman who has the dress and deportment of the nobility.

It is unlikely that history has ever before seen a gathering like this, across the ravine-like barriers of class, race and culture which had divided human society since it left the caves. It is obviously no ordinary gathering, connected with business, art or pleasure. It is in fact a regular Sunday evening meeting of the Christian Church in Rome.

They had met earlier that day, at dawn, to celebrate the eucharist as a memorial of the death of Jesus. That had been a larger gathering, drawing Christians from all over the city, and presided over by several distinguished elders. This evening meeting, however, is an 'area' one, paralleled in other parts of the city by similar groups, who meet to pray and to be instructed in what they call 'the apostles' teaching'. This involves a good deal of learning by heart and reciting aloud various sayings and stories about Jesus, and hymns which summarise the basic beliefs of the Church:

> God was manifested in the body,
> Vindicated in the spirit,
> Seen by angels,
> Proclaimed among the nations,
> Believed in throughout the world,
> Glorified in highest heaven.[1]

However, it is the stories and sayings of Jesus which are of greatest interest to us today. Most of the Christians in Rome had been converted to the faith through personal contact with a believer, perhaps a neighbour, or someone they had met in the market or at work. The initial attraction, we can be sure, was the lifestyle and character of the Christians, who were, on all the evidence, calm, confident and compassionate people in the midst of a confused, miserable and often brutal world.

Soon, however, they will have discovered that the real distinguishing feature of these Christians was their belief that Jesus of Nazareth, a Jewish prophet of the previous generation, was the 'Son of God'. It was their conviction, too, that Jesus was alive, having risen from the dead after his crucifixion by the Roman authorities, and that he was in some way 'with' them, or 'in' them, or 'among' them.

Naturally, a group whose beliefs centred so totally on a single historical person would value above anything else whatever record was available to them of his words and the events of his life.

In fact, the only 'records' available to them were those often-repeated sayings and stories. From the earliest days of the Church, when it was first necessary to teach converts about Jesus, it had been the practice to get them to memorise his teaching. This teaching was known in Greek (the common language of the Church) as the *didache*.

People were converted through the Gospel (literally,

'good news'), the preaching of the central truth of the death of Jesus and his resurrection. This Gospel, also almost certainly retained in a simple, memorable form of words, was known as the *kerygma*, which means the word preached. We have in Paul's first letter to the Corinthians, written a couple of years before our imagined meeting in Rome, one of the forms in which this *kerygma* was passed on: 'I handed on to you the facts which had been imparted to me,' Paul wrote[2], and then he set out those 'facts', the essential core of the Christian gospel: 'Christ died for our sins in accordance with the Scriptures; was buried; and was raised to life on the third day, according to the Scriptures.'

But once people had accepted that 'core', a process of instruction began, which, by this time, culminated in their public baptism and acceptance into the Church. Much of this instruction undoubtedly consisted of committing to memory the *didache*: various sayings and actions of Jesus, together with other credal-like summaries of doctrine, as we have seen. They learnt them by heart because they were not yet written down, and in any case many if not most of the Christians would have been unable to read.

The church at Rome was particularly favoured to have had, for some years, a number of leaders who had known or met Jesus: Peter, of course, died there, and may have led the church for a time; and there was also Mark, who is generally identified with the young man who fled, leaving behind his tunic, on the occasion of the arrest of Jesus. He was a native of Jerusalem – the disciples met in his mother's house – and had been a companion of Paul. Presumably Peter and Mark 'filled out' the oral accounts with their own recollections of Jesus, but all the evidence (and it is massive) is that these sayings and stories were sacrosanct, and that the form of words in which they were recorded was passed on with meticulous attention to verbal accuracy.

That is not surprising, given the circumstances. Naturally the Church did not want its primary sources corrupted. Equally, those who had newly committed themselves to a dynamic, controversial and potentially revolutionary faith would want to ensure that what they were now living and preparing to die for was the authentic thing and not an embellished or distorted version. So they would learn the words carefully, and pass them on carefully, too. It is remarkable to recognise the style and manner of Jesus in the traditions of churches as far apart as Caesarea, Antioch and Rome, as they appear in the various Gospels associated with these places.[3]

So these recorded sayings and stories –which were found in many of the centres of the Christian Church in the first century – can be regarded as a reliable record of what the early Church believed. More than that, they undoubtedly reflect many of the authentic words and actions of Jesus.

It was such a record which would have been available to Mark in Rome when he set out some time in the sixties AD to compile his Gospel. Clearly it was felt that the time had come to commit these things to writing. Perhaps, until then, the Christians had believed that the second coming of Jesus (what they called the *parousia*) was to be so soon that books about his first coming would be instantly out of date. They may well have seen the future of the Church as only to be reckoned in years, not decades or centuries; not such a period as would need a written book to enshrine its Founder's teaching.

But as the years and decades passed the decision was taken, in various of the Church centres around the Roman world, to commit their oral records to parchment, so that if the return of Jesus was to be delayed beyond the lifetime of the eye-witnesses of his ministry, a permanent record would be available, bearing their guarantee of authenticity.

The Christians in Rome would have been very well placed for such a project. Peter was (or had been) available, and so was John Mark; and they had a carefully-preserved collection of sayings and stories.

On that basis, we may presume, Mark set about his work, increasingly aware as he did so that the tide of opposition and even persecution was moving in on the church at Rome. This reached a peak after AD 65, when Nero made the Christians the scapegoats for a fire which devastated the city.

When we read his Gospel today with this background in mind we can see a great deal of internal evidence for it. Many commentators have noted the almost breathless pace of his narrative – the most common adverb in the first few chapters is 'immediately'. One story leads swiftly into the next. There hardly seems time to reflect on one event before another is being reported.

Much of Mark's Gospel, of course, is the same as Luke's, in substance and even in language. But when something occurs in Mark which is uniquely his, a story, a phrase or a piece of information not found in any other Gospel, it is often obvious that only Peter could have provided it.

It may be worthwhile to look at a few examples. In Mark 1:36, he records that 'Simon and those who were with him' went after Jesus when he retired to a desert place to pray, and told him that the crowds were looking for him. That little piece of information is unique to Mark's Gospel. So is a fascinating addition to the strange story of the cursing of the fig tree[4], where Mark alone records that it was Peter who noticed that the tree had indeed withered.

In much the same way, though it was something Peter would surely rather have forgotten, Mark alone adds several touches of detail to the story of the apostle's denial of Jesus in the high priest's courtyard: that Peter was 'warming himself at the fire', that the cock crowed the first time after his first, hesitant denial, and that his tears of remorse came when 'back into his mind came the words of Jesus'.

In fact, on virtually every occasion when Mark records something that the other Gospels omit it is a detail that could only have been known to a close associate of Jesus or an eye-witness of the events: that the palsied man was carried by 'four' men; that the name of the blind beggar in Jericho was Bartimaeus; that the disciples were 'amazed' at the way Jesus led them up to Jerusalem; that when the rich young ruler told Jesus that he had always kept the commandments Jesus 'looking at him, loved him'; that it was in the house at Capernaum that the disciples disputed as to which of them was the greatest.

These, and many more examples, seem to provide convincing evidence that Mark had access to the recollections of an intimate disciple of Jesus and an eye-witness of the events – presumably Peter[5] – as well as the orally transmitted source material. From the two, he produced his Gospel, the shortest, most concise but, as we have seen, most intimate of the first three Gospels – the 'synoptic' Gospels, as they are known, because it was thought that they looked at the life of Jesus through a single 'eye'.

One other fascinating problem remains as far as Mark's Gospel is concerned, and that is its ending. All textual scholars agree that the Gospel, as originally written, ended at what we now know as Chapter 16, verse 8. The disciples, having found the empty tomb of Jesus, fled from the scene 'and said nothing to anyone, for they were afraid'.

It is a strange place to end – even stranger when one considers that the last word in the sentence in Greek is a conjunction which grammar ordains should never be employed to end a sentence, let alone a whole book. People have speculated that Mark may have been arrested before he could finish the final paragraphs of his Gospel; or that he had a heart attack as he was writing; or, more prosaically, that the final page of his book was lost. What seems to be beyond doubt is that the ending to Mark's Gospel as printed in the older translations was in fact added by someone in the second century to provide a more suitable and comprehensive finish to the book, in line with Matthew and Luke.

So Mark wrote his Gospel, and we have it today as the earliest 'biography' of Jesus. We owe its existence not only to its author, as we have seen, but also to Peter, as an eye-witness of the 'event', and also to innumerable ordinary and long-forgotten Christians in Rome (and before that in Palestine) whose memorising of the stories and sayings of Jesus, recited over and over again and handed on with meticulous care to their successors, has given us this priceless record of Jesus of Nazareth.

# 4

# THE GOSPELS AS EVIDENCE

So far, we have frequently referred to 'the Gospels', and seen, in reconstruction, how one of them (Mark) probably came to be written. The time has now come to look at them more closely. Most people have heard of their names, if only because of the old rhyme:

> Matthew, Mark, Luke and John,
> Bless the bed that I lie on.

Of the four, Mark is undoubtedly the oldest, and the accepted datings for the others make Luke the next oldest, then Matthew and finally, some time later, John. Matthew, Mark and Luke are very similar. They are referred to as the 'synoptic' Gospels because they have a common outline. Indeed, whole tracts of them are identical, down to the most insignificant parenthesis, giving rise to the belief that they must have had a common written source.

In fact, it is not quite as simple as that. Textual scholars have established to their own satisfaction − and that of almost everybody else − that Mark is not only the first Gospel, but is also the basis of the other two synoptic Gospels. In other words, their compilers had Mark in front of them and used large parts of it word for word as the skeleton of their own books.

However, that only accounts for about half of Luke and Matthew. Of the rest, more than two hundred verses are virtually identical in Matthew and Luke, although they do not appear in Mark. Most of these are sayings of Jesus − about John the Baptist, about the lawyers and Pharisees, about the future and about the way his disciples should conduct themselves. These facts have led to the theory that Matthew and Luke both had access to a second written source, which the scholars have called 'Q' − from the

German word for 'source', *Quelle* – and which they think originated at Antioch.

That still leaves three hundred verses in Matthew and four hundred in Luke which are 'original' – that is to say, they are not to be found anywhere else. Most of this material in Matthew has a distinctly Jewish flavour, and it is this part of his Gospel which may well have come from the church in Jerusalem and even, indeed, from the 'Matthew' who gives it its name, the tax-collector who became a disciple of Jesus.

The 'original' material in Luke is mostly in the middle chapters of the Gospel, and includes some of the best-known parables of Jesus, including the Good Samaritan and the Prodigal Son. No one would dispute that these have the authentic flavour of Jesus about them, even though they do not appear in any of the other Gospels. It is widely assumed that Luke gathered this material while he was at Caesarea during Paul's imprisonment, between AD 57–59, presumably from an oral tradition preserved in the church there.

So we can begin to picture how the three Gospel writers compiled their books. Mark worked at Rome, as we have seen, using the local oral tradition supplemented by the evidence of eye-witnesses, including Peter. 'Matthew' used Mark, plus 'Q' and other material, possibly from the Jerusalem church, but probably compiled his Gospel at Antioch. Luke also used Mark and 'Q', but supplemented them with material he had obtained at Caesarea and also, possibly, from Mary the mother of Jesus, as we shall see later.

The inverted commas around 'Matthew' are there because we simply do not know the identity of the book's final compiler; but, as we have seen, there may well be some material which came into the church at Jerusalem from the apostle Matthew himself.

So the three synoptic Gospels took shape, and were in the hands of the Church by about AD 70. The fourth Gospel, John's, we shall be considering in more detail later on. All four Gospels were included without argument in the 'canon' of the New Testament when it was finally established by the Church centuries later, but they have been recognised and revered as 'holy writ' from the earliest days of Christianity.

This makes it all the more surprising that many believers, as well as unbelievers, are not really familiar with their contents. It could be that those who have turned to them have found them surprising, disconcerting even, and have decided that close study of them — as distinct from devotional or liturgical reading — is best left to the experts.

But they are not, at first sight, very complicated or obscure books. The fourth Gospel is certainly profound, sometimes mystical, but the other three have all the appearances of straight-forward narrative. However, the thoughtful reader will soon find himself asking questions. The opening chapters of Matthew, if he starts at the beginning of the New Testament, will immediately pose problems for the modern reader, with a distinctly strange genealogy tracing Jesus's ancestry back to Abraham, followed by an account of the birth of Jesus which in almost every detail is completely different from that offered by St Luke.

Then, as the reader goes further into the narrative, he may well become aware that this is not biography as we understand it today. The events in Matthew, for instance, appear to be dictated not by chronological order, but by the desire to create a 'pattern' of teaching and events, in clearly marked off sections, each ending with the same verbal formula: 'When Jesus had finished these sayings . . .' Matthew also seems obsessively concerned with relating every single event and saying of Jesus to an Old Testament prophecy, often one which by the normal criteria of interpretation has nothing whatever to do with the subject.

It is at this point that the careful reader may begin to lose heart. He has turned to the Gospels to find out about Jesus, but is now unsure how to regard what he is reading. Is it meant to be history? Is it an extended sermon? Is it a mixture of legendary material with a base of historical fact? Or is it some other way of communicating a 'message' which is not biography or history (though it contains both) but which tells a story about a person that is true in a sense that 'mere' history or biography can never be?

Most of the experts now would choose the last of those options. Not long ago (such are the shifts of scholarly opinion) many would have selected the second or third options, regarding the Gospels either as a message presented through myth or as very dubious history distorted by the passage of time and the emendations of over-enthusiastic believers.

Probably the simplest and most straight-forward approach for the 'ordinary' reader is none of these, but simply to regard the four Gospels as biographies. However, they are not biographies as the twentieth century knows them. They are the products of a culture and a world-view vastly different from our own, and need to be read through different 'spectacles' if we are to avoid misunderstanding them.

Even the most casual reader will see that there is a vast difference between the first three and the fourth Gospel. But there is also more difference between Matthew, on the one hand, and Mark and Luke on the other, than would appear at first, and that difference can best be expressed in terms of their aims. We have already seen a little of what Mark set out to do, but the time has come to look at the work of the 'historian' of the Gospel authors, Luke.

He was a doctor, the 'beloved physician' referred to by Paul[1], a Greek who was Paul's companion on several of his missionary journeys. He tells us, in the prologue to his Gospel, exactly what he was setting out to do:

> Many authors have undertaken to draw up an account of the events that have happened among us, following the traditions handed down to us by the original eyewitnesses and servants of the Gospel. And so I in my turn, as one who has gone over the whole course of these events in detail, have decided to write a connected narrative for you, so as to give you authentic knowledge about the matters of which you have been informed.

That is the most unambiguous declaration of intent

offered by any of the biblical authors. Luke was, as he implies, well aware of the plethora of biographical and quasi-biographical material about Jesus which was available to the Christian churches of his day. But, as an educated man and a shrewd observer, he was also undoubtedly aware of the danger of the growth of a Jesus cult, based on legends and hearsay, and the uncritical acceptance of every story and saying of Jesus then current in the Church. There were certainly many such stories and sayings, some of them known to us now, many presumably lost when they failed to gain official approval later on.

Luke took upon himself the daunting task of sorting through all of this material, checking sources, looking for corroboration and, we must assume, interviewing eye-witnesses. Such, at any rate, is the claim of this prologue.

Now this is, in essence, the role of the genuine historian. His aim is simple: to give his readers as reliable and accurate an account of past events as his research, skill and judgment can produce. If Luke sets out to do this, and if his other work suggests that he had the integrity and ability to do it, then here we may expect to find as near to the definitive history of Jesus as we are likely to get anywhere.

Does his 'other work' suggest this? The only other work we have from his pen is the book known as the 'Acts of the Apostles', Luke's account of the history of the infant Church from the time of the resurrection until Paul's captivity in Rome — about thirty years. Acts is a fascinating book which has not been subjected to the kind of minute analysis that scholars have given to the Gospels. However, all the recent work done on it suggests that where details can be verified, Luke has got them right — places, people, titles, customs and dates. His intention here, as in his Gospel, was to provide an orderly, chronological and reliable account of events, and in the process he has given us one of the most vivid and readable pictures of life in the Roman Empire of his time.

The great archaeologist, Sir William Ramsay, has played a major part in establishing Luke's credentials as an historian. There was a time when some scholars, especially certain German theologians, cast doubt on Luke's reliability. They described Acts as an *eirenikon*, a propaganda document written with the intention of glossing over divisions in the early Church (notably between Peter and Paul) and presenting it as a united, divinely-ordered force. However, William Ramsay's work proved beyond any doubt, as A.M. Hunter puts it, that Acts is

> not an historical romance, or a book of legends, or a third-rate chronicle, but a first-rate history in which the narrative shows marvellous truth, not only in its broad outlines but even in the smallest details − like the titles of the local magistrates in Thessalonica ('politarchs'), or the Mediterranean Labours, or the customs and legends current in various places like Lystra.[2]

Today, the historical accuracy of Acts is universally accepted by New Testament scholars, and the *eirenikon* theory has been generally discarded.

Luke's sources for Acts are easier to establish than those for his Gospel. In the latter part of the book (Chapters 16–28) he had his own travel-diary, sometimes quoted verbatim in the famous 'we' passages[3] and, of course, he had Paul as an informant. In the earlier part of the book he is relating events which happened before he became personally involved; but we may safely assume that Peter and John Mark were his sources for the first five chapters, and that Philip, with whom Luke stayed for many days in Caesarea[4], was the informant for events in that area. Luke himself may well have been a native of Antioch. In any case, we know that he spent some time there, and presumably based his account of events in the church at Antioch on personal knowledge or eye-witnesses.

All of this confirms that Luke is not a casual or careless story-teller, but a hard-working and conscientious historian. When he turned his attention to chronicling the early Church he had already finished his Gospel. But the same approach, the same careful attention to detail, is evident in the earlier book, too.

That is not to say, of course, that Luke is infallible as an historian. Such a degree of certainty is simply unattainable. Occasionally in his Gospel one suspects either that he has made a mistake (as, for instance, with the dates of Quirinius and his census[5]) or that he has incorporated material which he did not fully understand or could not possibly verify (for example, the genealogy in Chapter 3). Equally, one must say that the first century's idea of an historical narrative is not precisely the same as ours, so that our criteria of 'accuracy' are sometimes inappropriate as tests of his work.

But this does not in any way seriously undermine Luke's value as a chronicler, and to any attempt at reconstructing the 'Jesus of history' he is an important, and perhaps the most important, contributor.

On the other hand, Matthew probably offers less than the other three Gospels to that task, mainly because his objective is predominantly persuasion rather than information. As we have seen his Gospel is essentially 'Jewish' in flavour, and it is usually assumed that its most distinctive elements originated in the church of Jerusalem. However, although he uses the same source – 'Q' – as Luke for many of the sayings and stories of Jesus, his arrangement of the material is not that of the historian, even the first-century historian. Matthew is a persuader, he is arguing a case; and to drive it home he draws not only upon all the available stories, pronouncements and sayings of Jesus, but also scores of Old Testament prophecies which he is at immense pains to demonstrate refer to Jesus and prove he is the Messiah.

I have already said that no one is very certain about the identity of the author, or compiler, of Matthew. Papias, early in the second century, refers to Matthew − the tax-collector who was called to be a disciple and an apostle − as having written the *'Logia'* in Hebrew. *'Logia'* means 'sayings' or 'oracles', and could well describe the heart of the first Gospel, which offers much more of the direct teaching of Jesus than Mark or Luke. However, the reference to 'Hebrew' is baffling, as the Gospel of Matthew quotes the Jewish Scriptures in Greek, from the Septuagint version. The difference is apparent even in translation – the Septuagint gives at times a quite different version of a passage. It is unlikely, to say the least, that a Jew from Jerusalem, like Matthew, would have chosen to use the Greek Septuagint for his Old Testament quotations, and, of course, it apparently contradicts the statement of Papias that he wrote the 'Sayings' in Hebrew.

However, the Papias reference does suggest that Matthew the apostle is a source, and perhaps a primary source, for part of the first Gospel. It could well be that his 'Sayings' were preserved in the Jerusalem Church and were eventually edited, together with the other material from 'Q' and elsewhere, into the Gospel as we now have it, by an anonymous compiler, some time between AD 65 and 75.

Matthew's is the longest and in some respects the most comprehensive of the Gospels. He sets out to demonstrate that Christianity is the consummation of Judaism and that Jesus, the Messiah, fulfils the Old Testament prophecies perfectly. Any honest reader would have to admit that at times Matthew seems to strain the evidence. The connection between some of the prophecies he quotes and the events and sayings of Jesus is in places somewhat tenuous, and in one place he quotes a 'prophecy' which simply does not exist in the Old Testament as we now have it.[6]

His Gospel opens with a kind of 'prologue' in the form of a story which sets the birth of Jesus in two contrasted dimensions. On the one hand, he is the true son of Abraham and David. A lengthy genealogy, much loved in the ancient world, testifies to this, and also achieves the kind of numerical pattern which seems to have fascinated Matthew – fourteen generations from Abraham to David, fourteen more from David to the exile, and finally fourteen from the exile to the birth of Jesus. There also appears to be a complicated 'cypher' worked into the genealogy based on the numerical value of the name 'David'.

Simply to relate such things is to demonstrate how far Matthew is from the modern idea of an historian. We could not imagine a Gibbon, a Trevelyan or a Taylor adapting or arranging names and dates so that they formed mathematical patterns or provided intricate word clues to some mystical inner meaning. To the modern reader it is strange, perhaps even baffling; but it was a common-place of the culture in which Matthew wrote, and we are simply adopting a kind of historical obscurantism if we refuse to recognise it and insist on reading him as though he were a modern historical 'reporter'.

This is equally true of the second 'dimension' in which Matthew sets his prologue. Just as Jesus is the son of Abraham, a Jew for Jews, so also he is a king for the whole of mankind. So, to his home in Bethlehem, chosen and prophesied birthplace of the Messiah, come the Eastern magi – wise men, astrologers – the colourful representatives of the wealth and wisdom of the Gentile world. And at the feet of a Jewish infant, the Messiah, they lay their precious gifts of gold, incense and myrrh.

It need neither surprise nor worry us that this story, so rich and so radical in its meaning, was apparently unknown to Luke, whose own birth narrative, probably based on Mary's own recollections[7], presents an entirely different account of the events. It was a common-place of Jewish devotional writing at that time to weave such imaginative stories around familiar prophecies, to give substance and flesh to what were otherwise elusive concepts. The literary form – a midrash – would have been familiar to the Jewish Christians in Jerusalem, for whom the story was probably first written; but there is no denying that it does not travel well, and has led to a good deal of misunderstanding and confusion when taken in a more literal and less imaginative sense by readers in other cultures and later times.

Matthew is an incomparable source, however, for the sayings of Jesus, and to him we owe the record of the magnificent Sermon on the Mount which has all the hall-marks of the authentic message of Jesus. Many parables are also preserved for us in the first Gospel and a great deal of the teaching of Jesus about the people of God, the Temple and, particularly, the Law. The material is again arranged, not chronologically, but in a pattern, with parables and sayings grouped in numerical sequences and the whole carefully framed to present the book as a parallel to the Old Testament Law and the prophets, of which its author sees it as the logical fulfilment.

So we have three basically similar Gospels, Matthew, Mark and Luke, each offering us a portrait of Jesus. There is, of course, a fourth Gospel, John, but I want to save him for later. For the present, the groundwork having been laid, the time has come to attempt the central task I have set myself in this book: to reconstruct from those first three Gospels, and the other contemporary material available to us, the life and message of Jesus. This will not, of course, be the Jesus of faith. That, I hope, will follow. For now, as carefully as we can, and claiming no more than can reasonably be deduced from the texts and all the meticulous work done on them by scholars, we shall try to see with new eyes the Jesus of history.

# 5

## JESUS COMES TO JORDAN

The stony banks of the River Jordan near Jericho might seem an unlikely setting for the birth of the most far-reaching religious movement in human history. The year was AD 29, the fifteenth year of the reign of Tiberius Caesar, and the event itself was probably regarded as unremarkable by most of those who witnessed it.

For some years a Jewish prophet, John, had been preaching a revivalist message and baptising those who responded to it in the shallow waters of the Jordan. His message was, it appears, new: not in its language or style but in its content.

In style John was like many who had gone before him in that painful period of Jewish history. Like them he used the language of the Law and the Prophets; like them he called his hearers to turn from false gods and submit themselves again to the righteous and holy rule of God. Like them he warned that only repentance could deliver them from the servitude to other nations which had weighed upon them for more than three centuries.

So much was familiar to the Jews. The Zealots, the nationalist activists, believed that, as God alone is king, no other ruler had the right to reign over his people. They had toured the country areas for many years, recruiting young men for their liberation movement and preaching that God was calling the people *now* to deliver themselves from tyranny. A necessary preparation for that was total commitment to the *Torah*, the Law. God would fight for them and overthrow the hated Roman oppressors and their local puppets – but only if they demonstrated their complete loyalty to him.

Again, from time to time the tiny villages on the northern shores of the Dead Sea and up into the fertile Jordan valley would be visited by men with a different, though superficially similar, message. These were the Essenes, the semimonastic order of Jewish 'monks' who lived in the caves above the sea shore. It was their writings, and their copies of the scriptures, that were found by a shepherd in 1947 and became known as the Dead Sea Scrolls. They too preached that the time had come for throwing off the Roman yoke, but they believed that this military struggle must be complemented by a cleansing of the community and its worship. They had themselves withdrawn from secular life to form what they believed was a pure community, one in which God was already the undisputed king. This would act as a model for the wider community of Israel when it was liberated.

They had withdrawn, but only in order eventually to advance. Their dwelling was in desert caves, but their objective was, like the Zealots, nothing less than to recapture biblical Israel for Jehovah. Only their doctrinal emphasis was different. There would have to be a struggle, because the holy community God desired could not exist alongside the abominations of the Gentiles. For the Zealots, now was the time for the sword; for the Essenes, now was the time for spiritual purification and renewal.

To the village people the differences probably seemed academic. Both of them spoke of the need for a 'pure Israel' and both called them to forge a closer link between the religion of their fathers and the land which God had given them — and which the Greeks, first, and now the Romans had stolen by force.

When John — nicknamed the 'Baptiser' — came, he probably seemed at first to speak the same message. But as people listened, they detected a different note. The Zealots and the Essenes were essentially nationalists. Their message was concerned with the liberation and purification of Israel. But John invited his hearers to take a broader view.

For him, there was nothing particularly valuable about being a Jew, in the sense of being a descendant of Abraham. 'Why,' he scornfully pointed out, 'God could create sons of Abraham from these stones.' It was not race or birth that mattered, but behaviour. He did not see the *Torah* (the Law) as a banner to be waved in support of nationalism, but as an expression of universal ethical values.

So, to their great surprise, he addressed his message not only to Jews, but also to Roman soldiers, calling them, too, to repent and 'be content with their wages'. For John, judgment would fall not just on the Romans and their allies, but on Israel, too. God's winnowing fan was in his hand, and the process of sorting out the good wheat from the useless chaff was about to begin. In John's message there was a kind of universal urgency. It was not simply that it was time to deliver Israel from bondage. Rather, it was high time for repentance, for judgment was at the very door, knocking for admittance, and that judgment was for all, Jew or Gentile, chosen or not chosen.

The sins John denounced were not the ritual sins which so concerned the Essenes (and the Pharisees, whom we shall consider later) — breaking the food laws or the Sabbath, or failing to observe ceremonies or denounce the blasphemies of the Gentiles or Samaritans. John was more concerned with personal sins: selfishness, financial dishonesty, sexual immorality, injustice. 'The man with two tunics should share with him who has none, and the one who has food should do the same.'

But behind this homespun morality loomed the impending storm of God's judgment: 'The axe is already at the root of the trees . . . Who warned you to flee from the coming wrath?' Strangely, although he called the crowds who thronged to hear him a 'brood of vipers', the more he denounced them and their sins, the more they flocked to the Jordan to sit at his feet.

Some undoubtedly felt that he could be the Messiah. The activities of the Zealots, the preaching of the Essenes and the generally frustrated mood of the Jewish people had combined to create an enormous sense of expectancy. The previous thirty or forty years had seen several false alarms, with one religious or revolutionary leader after another emerging to claim an enthusiastic following and start rumours that this was the long-promised Deliverer.

But John was sufficiently different from the others to fuel such hopes on a grander scale, and when he took to baptis-

ing those who came to him many felt that they were indeed
in at the birth of a new age.

Baptism was a familiar enough ritual to the Jews, of
course. The Essenes practised it, and so did the Pharisees – a
ritual washing to signify a new start, a renunciation of the
past and the embracing of a new commitment. But John
gave it a fresh urgency. He combined it with the idea of
fleeing from God's judgment and preparing oneself for his
soon-coming Kingdom.

The 'Kingdom' was an idea widely preached in the Judaism of the time and it was usually associated with submitting
to the strict rules and traditions taught by the Rabbis. The
regular Jewish prayers of this period emphasise the need to
sever oneself from all that is outside the realm of God's rule
(including, of course, Gentile practices) and follow the set
prayers and rituals meticulously, in order to avoid pollu-
tion. In that way the 'Kingdom' would be restored.

In contrast, John's message was starkly clear: 'Do not
begin to say to yourselves, "We have Abraham as our
father" '[1] – that is, do not hide behind your Jewish religion
and ancestry – but turn from sin and renew your desire for
holiness by accepting baptism. What John called them to
was not a retreat into traditional Judaism but an advance
into a new kind of religious commitment. It was probably
this that made people feel he could be the Messiah.

However, John explicitly rejected that idea. Indeed,
more dramatically, he described himself as a fore-runner, a
kind of one-man advance party preparing the way for the
Messiah.

'I baptise you with water,' John told the crowds. 'But
one more powerful than I will come, the thongs of whose
sandals I am not worthy to untie. He will baptise you with
the Holy Spirit and with fire.' And he applied to himself the
words of Isaiah: 'A voice of one calling in the desert,
Prepare the way for the Lord.'

So the occasion in AD 29 when John met Jesus by the
River Jordan, and baptised him, was a momentous one for
them both. From that moment, it seems, John urged his
own disciples to follow Jesus: 'He must increase, but I must
decrease.'

It is natural to wonder whether John knew Jesus, or at any rate knew about him, before this meeting. According to Luke they were related through their mothers[2], though John came from the Judaean hill country and Jesus from Galilee. Jesus would certainly have known about John – everybody did. And as a devout Jew, brought up in what was undoubtedly a deeply religious home, it is highly likely that he had shared in the teaching and activities of one or other of the 'revivalist' movements of the time. We can assume that the qualities of eloquence and leadership which he later displayed were already becoming evident, so that as perceptive a person as John might be expected to have noticed him, at the very least.[3]

However, there are various clues and hints which suggest a much deeper connection between them. Although in the Gospels there is no suggestion that Jesus had been a disciple of John (rather the contrary), there is so much in common between their style of preaching, and indeed its content in the ethical field, that at the least we must assume a common source, if not actual collaboration at some stage.

It is not simply that they both sound like the rabbis of the time. It is much more that they do not. They both use some of the words and phrases coined by the Essenes, and now familiar to scholars through the Dead Sea Scrolls, but they also both take the liberty of using them at times in a radically different way. Jesus, of course, did this much more daringly, but several of his most distinctive ideas are at any rate hinted at, or 'pre-echoed', in the teaching of John.

John's preaching of judgment and purification has obvious associations with the Essenes (and the Zealots and Pharisees), but he broadened it, as we have seen, far beyond the confines of the *Torah*: and Jesus gave it a cosmic interpretation.[4]

The phrase 'the kingdom of heaven' was also common to the other religious revival movements of the time, but possibly John, and certainly Jesus, gave it a totally new dimension. The idea of a 'covenant' people is fundamental to the Essenes, and Jesus gives that, too, a new meaning. And the idea of the Messiah as a 'suffering Servant', first found in Isaiah, recurs powerfully in the Dead Sea Scrolls (related to the 'Teacher') and, of course, is worked out, step by step, in Jesus's understanding of his own death for us and 'for the glory of the Father'.

It would not be surprising to discover evidence one day that Jesus (and John) had spent time with the Essenes in their community by the Dead Sea. After all, Jesus was at least thirty when John baptised him, and although we know he was described as a carpenter[5], and undoubtedly plied that trade, we may also assume that he spent his early adult years in some kind of theological and spiritual preparation for his ministry. At any rate, there is no evidence to suggest that he was taken by surprise when his baptism was seen to open a public ministry for him, which included the gathering of a corps of personal disciples. It is related in the Gospels as the start of his ministry, but in a way which clearly implies that it was an inevitable stage in the vocation of an exceptionally gifted person, not the sudden, unexpected election of an unknown from the country.

The baptism of Jesus at the hands of John, however, is seen by the Gospel writers as the inauguration of his public ministry. It is also seen as some kind of divine endorsement of it. The Old Testament frequently relates how its great figures — men like David, Elijah and Ezekiel — were given a special gift of the Spirit of God for the tasks to which Jehovah had called them. Now the Gospel writers see Jesus in the same light. He was already a godly man, but at this moment, they claim, he received the special gift of the Spirit which marked him out as the Son of God. All three record the 'voice from the sky' which followed his baptism: 'This is my Son, whom I love; with him I am well pleased.' They are *not* saying, as some modern theologians argue, that he *became* the 'Son of God' at that moment, but that his baptism was the moment when his true identity was first revealed.

Now this obviously creates a problem for the reader of the Gospels. If a voice from heaven was clearly heard by the crowds alongside the River Jordan stating quite unambiguously that Jesus was God's beloved Son, why did even his disciples not come to that understanding of him until much later – probably almost two years later, by their own accounts?[6] And how does this highly public pronouncement square with the repeated insistence of Jesus in the earlier part of his ministry that those who had discovered his true identity were not to spread it abroad – the so-called 'messianic secret'?[7]

The answer must surely lie in the historical perspective of the Gospel writers. They were not taking shorthand notes on the banks of the Jordan and writing them up for the next morning's newspapers. Instead, they were handling material which had been passed on to them within the Christian Church since its inception, and trying to assess its importance and value to that Church as it preached the Gospel and taught its converts. Obviously there were several parallel accounts of the baptism of Jesus available to them, which differed in detail. But all agreed about three things: that Jesus was baptised by John; that 'the Spirit as a dove descended on him', and that a voice came out of heaven, saying 'This is my Son whom I love; with him I am well pleased.'

As a matter of history, the first of these statements is undoubtedly accurate. The other two do not lie in the area of historical analysis. They are, it seems to me, statements of faith. That is not to say that 'nothing' happened, but that the record we have of them is interpretation as well as reportage.

For instance, it may well be that a dove – the feathered kind, a bird – actually flew down at the time of the baptism, and even landed on Jesus's head. If that were so, to the eye of faith – then, or later – the Spirit had come 'as a dove' upon Jesus; and the proof of that was the ministry of Jesus which followed, not any tortuous arguments about the incarnation of the Holy Spirit in the form of a small bird.

Similarly we cannot tell now whether the 'voice' was of the kind that everyone present heard. Certainly on a later occasion when a Gospel records such a 'voice' the bystanders described it as a roll of thunder.[8] Such instances should warn us not to be too literal in our interpretation of 'events' like these. It may well be that the 'voice' was an inner conviction given to Jesus, and perhaps to John, that he was indeed the Son of God: a conviction later shared with the disciples and reported in the Gospels. It may be that there was some external sound, but not (it would seem) one that the bystanders could interpret as a clear message, or they would surely have accepted the messiahship of Jesus there and then. The 'fact', in historical terms, is the baptism. The gift of the Spirit, and the heavenly endorsement of Jesus's ministry, are statements of faith, even if they are based on events that actually happened.

So Jesus embarked on his ministry, and the detailed record of his actions and sayings begins. It is strange that we know so little about the first thirty years of his life, but all four Gospels, and the other historical references to him, concentrate upon the brief three years from his baptism at the Jordan to his execution in Jerusalem.

It is true, of course, that Luke and Matthew both include, as a kind of prologue to his biography, accounts of his birth in Bethlehem, which we shall consider in the next chapter; and Luke adds one fascinating story of a boyhood excursion to Jerusalem. Apart from that, the Gospels are silent about the intervening years, and consequently there have been many attempts, mostly completely speculative, at filling in the gaps.

One piece of speculation, however, seems likely to be true. When Jesus was still a young boy, perhaps in his early teens, there was an armed insurrection in Galilee, led by Judas of Gamala. The insurgents, fore-runners of the Zealots, captured Sepphoris for a few days, but the Roman general Varus put down the uprising, razed the town and crucified the rebels along the roadside. As all this occurred within walking distance of Nazareth, it seems virtually certain that Jesus knew of it, probably met people — relatives, perhaps — who had been involved in it, and even saw the bodies of the protesters hanging from the crosses where the Romans would have left them as a dreadful warning to other would-be revolutionaries.

Such an event — like, say, the hunger marches of the

Thirties – would have made an indelible impression on the memory of a young boy. It may have helped to shape Jesus's later, and very emphatic, rejection of violence as a way of changing things. It may have helped to turn him away from the various nationalistic movements, which almost gloried in such suicidal exploits. What it did *not* do, as we can clearly see in the Gospels, was to make him hate the Roman soldiers themselves. It was that magnanimity, that universal practice of forgiveness, which perhaps most clearly of all marked Jesus off from all his contemporaries.

# 6

# THE BIRTH OF JESUS

Most people are familiar with the story of the birth of Jesus: probably more familiar than they are with anything else in the Gospels. Carols and nativity plays have made the elderly Joseph, the young Mary, the stable, the star, the shepherds and the wise men part of the folklore of our culture. It is probably just as well that most people do not know how difficult it really is to fit those widely-accepted characters and events into any kind of coherent historical pattern.

Any serious attempt to establish the probable facts about the birth of Jesus has to begin with Luke, whose Gospel is generally regarded as historical in intention, and who does seem to have had access to Mary, the mother of Jesus, either in person, or indirectly. He sets the story very carefully against certain historical landmarks. Augustus was the Emperor and Quirinius was governor of Syria. It was during a census carried out by him that Mary and Joseph came to Bethlehem from their home town, Nazareth. Matthew tells us that the birth of Jesus took place during the reign of Herod; Luke says that Herod was king of Judaea at the time when Elizabeth conceived John, fifteen months before the birth of Jesus.

Immediately we have problems. Herod died in 4 BC and P. Sulpicius Quirinius became proconsul of Syria in AD 6, when he carried out a notorious census. This later date is in any case impossible for the birth of Jesus, because it is too late to tie in with the known date of the baptism of Jesus in AD 29, when he was, according to Luke, 'about thirty'. All the historical indications are that Jesus was born between 5 and 2 BC (as we now know it), and if we accept the tradition that Herod was king at the time, we must settle for 4 or 5 BC. This would make Jesus thirty-three or thirty-four at the time of his baptism, which is only 'about thirty' on the most liberal reckoning.

We can be reasonably certain, however, of the identity of his parents, Joseph and Mary, and that Joseph was probably older than Mary. She was still alive some time after the crucifixion of her son, about thirty-three years later, whereas Joseph was dead before Jesus began his public ministry.

Both Luke and Matthew give the place of birth as Bethlehem. Matthew implies that it was Joseph and Mary's home town, while Luke claims that they went there in obedience to a Roman census, because they were descendants of David and Bethlehem was 'David's city'. Both agree that some time after the birth of Jesus they moved to Nazareth: apparently for the first time (according to Matthew), but returning there, to their home (according to Luke).

The other thing they both agree about is that Mary conceived the child while she was still a virgin. In one sense, an 'event' of that kind is beyond rational verification and we accept or reject it on the basis of faith. On the other hand, it must be said that the evidence for it is strong. It was of course widely believed in the early Church, of which Mary herself was a member. And there are persistent hints in the Gospels and elsewhere that there was something 'abnormal' about the circumstances of the birth of Jesus. The insults of a Jewish crowd implied that he was illegitimate[1]; in Mark another crowd referred to him as the 'son of Mary', whereas the normal practice was to describe a boy as the son of his father, assuming one existed[2]. Of course, the historian requires exceptionally convincing evidence for an intrinsically unlikely event, and a virginal conception must come into that category. But when one says that the event cannot be proven, that is not at all the same thing as saying that it is unbelievable: a point to which we shall return in a later chapter.

So, what can we say about the birth of Jesus as an historical event? Clearly it happened: a man who lives must have been born. And clearly it must have happened just before the date that is now known as the start of a new era, the imaginary year 'zero'.

Assuming, as I think we must, that Luke is offering us a serious attempt at an historical account, based on the available evidence, we can place the birth at Bethlehem, and accept that the parents, Joseph and Mary, were there for a Roman census, though their home town was Nazareth. The difficulty over Luke's reference to Quirinius need not invalidate this: there were other and earlier censuses, and it is at least possible, from the evidence, that Quirinius, or his name-sake, had been proconsul of Syria at an earlier date.

It seems unlikely that the census took place under Herod the Great. The terms of his rule – but not of the succeeding 'Herods' – precluded such Roman activities. In that case, we can date the birth after 4 BC, which fits in more convincingly with the date of Jesus's baptism in AD 29. It is possible, as Luke mentions Herod with reference to the conception of John, but not in relation to the birth of Jesus, that the king had died in the meantime. If that were so, it would fix the birth of Jesus quite precisely, between 4 and 2 BC – fitting in very well with Luke's statement that Jesus was 'about thirty' in AD 29.

So we have the birth of Jesus at Bethlehem, to Mary, in circumstances that gave rise to rumours of illegitimacy. The parents were poor people. We know that from the offering which they made when Jesus was presented as a baby in the Temple – two doves, the permitted offering of the poor.

With regard to the other details of the birth narratives in the Gospels, there is no serious reason to reject Luke's report of the birth in a stable, because 'there was no room at the inn'; or of the shepherds who came to see the child. About Matthew's wise men, the flight into Egypt and the slaughter by Herod's soldiers of all the children in the area under two years of age, we may be permitted some historical scepticism. Most scholars do not think they were intended by their original author as records of historical events, but as a kind of animated anthology of Old Testament prophecies relating to the Messiah.[3]

However, one detail of Matthew's story may well have a basis in history, and that concerns the unusual star which the wise men saw 'in the east' and which led them to the infant 'King of the Jews'. Twice within the possible period of time there were exceptional conjunctions of stars. In 7 BC (a bit early for the probable birth date) there was a close conjunction of Jupiter and Saturn in Pisces which would have given the appearance of a single, abnormally bright star. And there was a series of unusual conjunctions in 3 − 2 BC, which would undoubtedly have attracted the attention of astrologers in the Middle East. It may be that these events were the starting point of the story of the Wise Men. An unusually bright star or exceptional constellation was remembered as occurring at about the time of the birth of Jesus, and this may well then have become an element in the *midrash* which the writer had set himself to create.

We only have one story about the boyhood of Jesus recorded in the Gospels, Luke's account of a visit to the Temple in Jerusalem. The family had, it seems, made the journey there from Nazareth in the north, together with friends and neighbours, rather like medieval pilgrims. When they were on the way home again, and a whole day into the journey, Joseph and Mary realised that Jesus was not in the party. They retraced their steps to the temple, and three days later found their twelve-year-old son sitting among the theologians, listening and asking questions. They rebuked him for causing them anxiety, to which (according to Luke) the boy answered, 'Wouldn't you have expected to find me in my Father's house?'

This is, by any standards, a remarkable answer, and it has led some people to question its authenticity. They feel that it could only have been phrased by someone who was aware of the Christian belief in the divinity of Jesus, and was intended to show that even as a boy he knew of his special relationship with God. This would be equally true of the translation offered by the King James Version: 'Wist ye not that I must be about my Father's business?' − a version rejected, incidentally, by every modern translator.

However, the story cannot be lightly dismissed. The incident itself has all the hallmarks of authenticity. The pilgrimage to Jerusalem by a village party is a piece of Jewish folk history that would probably not have been

known to Luke in the ordinary course of events. The details
he relates seem authentic. And the anxiety of the parents,
and Mary's rebuke, ring true: 'Why have you treated us
like this, my son? Here have your father and I been very
worried, looking for you everywhere!'

Jesus's reply picked up the reference to 'father' in what
could almost be taken as a correction of his mother: 'But
why were you looking for me? Didn't you know that I must
be in *my father's* house?'⁴ Luke reports that his parents 'did
not understand his reply', but that Mary 'treasured all these
things in her heart'. The implication obviously is that later,
much later, she recalled the words and also saw their meaning. Presumably we owe Luke's account of the words (and
their implied meaning) to her.

Now the 'meaning', seen through the perspective of
subsequent events and the beliefs of the Christian Church,
is clearly no less than that the young Jesus knew he was 'the
Son of God' and that Joseph was not his father. That, it
seems, was how Mary and the early Church understood his
words. So it is tempting to suggest that at the end of an
accurately recorded incident from the childhood of Jesus
this piece of dialogue got added, or altered, in order to
reinforce the ideas of the pre-existence, divinity and virginal conception of the Christ, as they were later taught by
the Church.

It is a tempting explanation, but it is not the only one, nor
necessarily the best.

It is at least as likely that these words were actually
spoken at the time and were correctly remembered by
Mary, but that at the time they were said they carried no
deeper significance than that Jesus, who was undoubtedly a
very devout young Jew, would have expected his parents to
look for him first in the Temple ('the Father's house'),
rather than the market or streets. Children often give puzz-
ling answers to simple question, as every parent knows. But
it is not surprising that Mary, remembering this remark
many decades later, should see in it deeper meanings about
her son.

Another reason for not lightly rejecting the authenticity

of this incident is its uniqueness. We have noted that it is the only story from the boyhood of Jesus recorded in the Gospels, but it is not by a long way the only such story that ever existed. A good number survive to this day in the pseudo-Gospels – the books which were rejected by the Church when the New Testament 'canon' was finalised.

Now if they survive today, and were known to the Church of the early centuries, then presumably some were known to Luke: probably, many. It is significant that he rejected all the boyhood stories of Jesus, *except this one*. Clearly Luke had some special reason for regarding this incident as authentic, and the most likely reason for that would be the corroboration of Mary. Certainly it has the feel of an eye-witness report in its detail and its dialogue. And if all the rest of the story is historical, including the dialogue, then it is probable that the answer of Jesus is accurately reported too.

Some people may wonder why I have not accepted the possibility, at least, that Jesus not only spoke the words, but also, at twelve years of age, was aware of their deeper significance. In fact, I do accept the possibility, but put it into the area of faith, with which I am not yet concerned. In attempting to reconstruct the history of Jesus, one can only say that the whole story, in word and action, sounds authentic. Between the misty stories of the birth of Jesus and the corroborated, clear history of his ministry, stands this one incident. It is a fascinating glimpse into the adolescence of a great man and a great figure of human history. Jesus did not suddenly 'happen' by Jordan in AD 29. In a small village of Galilee the carpenter's son was preparing himself, or being prepared, for his life's work. Who would doubt that intense and devoted study of the scriptures, and a love of the majestic Temple of Jehovah, would be essential parts of that preparation? And this story tells us that they were.

# 7

# WHAT WAS THE 'MESSAGE' OF JESUS?

If a twentieth-century Christian were to be transported in a time machine to first-century Judaea and found himself in a crowd listening to Jesus preaching, I suspect he would get a considerable shock. Even if he were fluent in Aramaic, and so could follow what was being said, he would still have some difficulty, I think, in fitting what he was hearing into the mental picture he had brought with him, based on his twentieth-century reading of the Gospels. Above all, he would be struck by the *Jewishness* of Jesus.

One of the great gifts of modern scholarship to our understanding of Jesus has been to re-discover the intense and all-pervading Judaism of his culture. To the crowds he was a rabbi, albeit a rather daring and innovative one. He used the rabbinical methods of teaching. He employed the idioms and figures of speech of the teachers in the synagogue. There is hardly an expression or phrase in the teaching of Jesus that cannot be found in the records of his contemporaries and predecessors.

He came from the wilderness, like all the great prophets of Israel — Moses, Elijah, Elisha and John the Baptist. He, like them, had a direct message from God, an uncompromising, demanding, searching message.

Like Jeremiah and Ezekiel, he used stories and acted parables to communicate his vision. Like Amos he denounced the corruption in society. Like Moses he offered them bread from heaven. Almost everything he said and did was firmly within the traditions of the religion and prophets of Israel. And almost all of it would fall with unfamiliar vibrations on the modern ear.

For instance, he constantly spoke of the 'kingdom of heaven' or the 'kingdom of God'. Indeed, you could say that it was the burden of his message. But today it is hard to grasp what a 'kingdom' is, so foreign is the very idea to modern Western thought.

The kingdom of God – his rule like an absolute monarch over his people – had been a popular theme in the decades before John the Baptiser and Jesus appeared on the scene. The Zealots and the Essenes spoke of it. John foretold it: the kingdom was 'at hand', the preparation for it was repentance and baptism.

But for Jesus, the 'kingdom' had arrived. 'If I, by the finger of God, cast out demons,' he told the Pharisees, 'then surely the kingdom of God is upon you.'[1] Do not waste time searching for messiahs, he advised the crowds: 'The kingdom of God is among you.'[2] In other words, not only had the kingdom come, but it had come *with him*. In some mysterious way, as John had been the fore-runner of the kingdom, so Jesus saw himself as representing its very presence. For three hundred years they had prayed and longed for God to visit and redeem his people, and now, said Jesus, he had done it.

Now this way of using a familiar Jewish 'theme' but yet giving it a completely new meaning seems to be typical of the teaching of Jesus. When we have absorbed the Jewishness of his teaching, we are ready to experience the 'shock of the new'. But if we do not appreciate the original meaning of the words and phrases he used, we shall miss the impact on his hearers of the shocking new twist he gave to them.

For the Jews of the first century, the 'kingdom of God' or the 'kingdom of heaven' were familiar phrases, clichés even. They referred to a future state of things when Israel had repented, the usurping invader had been expelled, and from the coast to the borders of the land, from 'Dan to Beersheba', Jehovah again ruled over his people in the perfect theocracy. They represented the final, decisive intervention of God in the history of his people, ushering in the golden age.

Various groups interpreted the way in which this would come about differently, as we have seen, but the fundamental idea was the same to all of them. Every pious Jew of the first century prayed for the coming of the kingdom, and according to his inclinations kept his sword polished or his prayer shawl unfolded.

John's preaching implied that the kingdom was imminent, that the decisive moment was at hand, and the crowds flocked to him because this was what they wanted more than anything else. After centuries of repression, God was about to vindicate them.

But then, towards the end of John's ministry, while the crowds were still thronging the banks of the River Jordan to hear him, the newly-baptised Jesus emerged from the desert with the most dramatic message of all – not that the kingdom was coming, but that it had come. At first, beyond doubt, the crowds assumed he meant that the kingdom *as they had always understood it* had come: that the deliverance of Israel and the restoration of the throne of David was imminent.

But slowly it dawned upon his hearers that Jesus, while he used the traditional 'kingdom' language, saw the kingdom of God in radically different terms. More than that: though he was steeped in the culture and religion of Israel, and sounded like a rabbi or a scribe (a teacher of the law), the religion he preached was totally new.

The crowds in Galilee who first heard the preaching of Jesus were mostly farming or fishing people. All their lives they had been pressed by the Zealots, the Pharisees, or the Essenes to 'seek the kingdom of God'. They were familiar with the basic idea of it, which was an extension of the concept of the monarchy, as originally given to Israel (and barbarously destroyed by Greek and Roman): that God's reign over his people was absolute, and that no foreign usurper could be allowed to take his place.

They were also familiar with the way the various 'parties' of contemporary Judaism saw it. In a period of intense national frustration, extreme solutions are usually preferred, and so it was in Galilee. The Pharisees pursued an almost fanatical search for 'purity', by which they meant total obedience to the *Torah* and the rejection of Gentile or pagan influences. The Essenes called for an equally intense commitment, but to be expressed more in terms of ritual – washings, baptisms, ritual meals – but equally aimed at defining the chosen people as Israel and making them fit subjects for God's kingly rule. And the Zealots – again, with uncompromising fervour – agitated for an armed struggle, to rid the land of the usurper and restore it to God.

Each party used the 'kingdom' as its slogan, and it may well be that by the time John came on the scene the ordinary people of Galilee were getting a little tired of it. That, at any rate, is the view of a scholar who has recently made a special study of the Judaism of this period.[3] The armed rebellions of the Zealots had all been crushed and the leaders executed – and the Romans were still in charge. The Essenes – the 'monks' from Qumran – may well have appeared rather remote from the ordinary daily life of village, farm and fishing boat. And the Pharisees, like the Puritans of seventeenth-century England, may well have seemed to have taken a good thing too far. The life of a tenant farmer was hard enough, without the constant pressure to pay tithes to the Temple in Jerusalem.

But the idea of the 'kingdom' remained. Although John does not appear to have used the phrase very much – there is just one reference to it on his lips, recorded by Matthew – the concept seems to have pervaded his preaching. Like the Pharisees, he associated it with moral purity; like the Essenes, he marked its preparation with baptism. But, as we have seen, his call went beyond Israel, which was a significant development, and for him morality was not so much a matter of observing the law, the *Torah*, as of inward reformation: 'Prove your repentance by the fruit it bears.'[4]

When Jesus appeared, there was no doubt of his message. It was the kingdom. 'Jesus came into Galilee preaching the gospel of God and saying, "The time has come; the kingdom of God is upon you; repent, and believe the gospel".' The 'gospel', of course, is simply 'good news'; so what Jesus was declaring, his hearers must have assumed, was that the deliverance the Zealots, the Essenes and the Pharisees had talked about – the 'good news' of the reign of God – had now arrived.

It is hardly surprising, then, that vast numbers flocked to hear him and, presumably, deserted John. At first, they must have wondered what was different. The language seemed familiar enough, though the emphasis was strange. Over the following months and years, as they heard his parables, saw his miracles, and watched him sharing meals with prostitutes and quisling employees of the foreign usurpers, they came to realise that he was not in fact at all like those who had gone before him.

The Zealots, Pharisees and Essenes all preached hatred against the enemies of Israel. All the Zealots had to offer the occupying Romans was a knife between the shoulder blades. To the Pharisees and Essenes, the Romans were under the curse of God. But Jesus, addressing the same crowds in Galilee, had different advice: 'What I tell you is this: Love your enemies and pray for your persecutors, *only so* can you be children of your heavenly Father.'[5] It is quite impossible to appreciate the shocking nature of this saying unless it is set against the prevailing mood of frustration and bitterness which vented itself in hatred of the Romans. The crowd would have had no difficulty at all in identifying the 'enemies' Jesus spoke of — the Gentiles who had systematically destroyed the power centres of the Jewish religion and, in the well-remembered past, blasphemed its holy sites and blasphemously flouted its laws.

One suspects that the crowd would also have had little difficulty in identifying the source of the advice which Jesus now urged them to reject. 'You have heard it said, "Love your neighbour, and hate your enemy".' *Who* had 'said'? The Zealots, the Pharisees and the Essenes, in their different ways. Each was concerned to define and rebuild the house of Israel. So, 'love your neighbour', providing he is a member of that house. Each was concerned to drive from the land the foreign Gentile. So, 'hate your enemy', the Roman occupier. Jesus could not have expressed more vividly, or more explicitly, how he differed from the other prophets and preachers of the day.

It was not as though Jesus simply called on the Jews to tolerate or accept their position, though that would have been shocking enough. He told them to *love* their enemies, to *love* the hated Romans: to pray for their persecutors and do them good. This was a strange notion of the kingdom!

Indeed, its very strangeness is the best proof of its authenticity – no one could have invented such a bizarre reversal of the prevalent doctrines.

Not only that, but Jesus practised what he preached. Later in his ministry he described the faith of a Roman centurion – an officer of that hated occupying army – as greater than anything he had found amongst the Jews.[6] So in word and action he reversed the code and practice of the time: 'You shall love your neighbour and *hate your enemy*'. In the teaching of Jesus, the enemy is the neighbour, and is to be loved. Only so can the kingdom come: 'Only so can you be the children of your heavenly Father.'

Jesus also reversed the interpretation of the kingdom favoured by the Pharisees. Their emphasis, as we have seen, was on 'purity'. The people of God, Israel, should purge from their lives and their society all that could be construed as compromise of the *Torah*. To achieve this, they set out with monumental dedication to fulfil every letter of the law, and, in the spirit of all such movements, interpreted it with greater and greater severity and attention to detail. In a memorable piece of irony, Jesus accused them of tithing mint, and at the same time ignoring 'weightier matters of the Law': 'You strain out a gnat, and swallow a camel!'[7] In other words, they observed the law over such minute details as offering to God one-tenth of their crop of mint (which was little more than a valueless weed), but ignored its major principles, such as caring for the weak and poor.

The Pharisees have had a bad press from Christians, largely because they appear to be the villains of the Gospels. This is itself almost certainly a misreading of the situation, however. There were 'good' Pharisees, like Nicodemus and those who tried to warn Jesus that Herod planned to kill him; and Jesus plainly sided with the Pharisees over the question of life after death.[8] Some biblical scholars, like Yaacov Fleming, of the Jerusalem Centre for Biblical Studies, believe that Jesus was closer to the Pharisees than to any other religious movement of the time. But there is no doubt that he was at pains to show how he differed from them over this whole concept of ritual or religious purity.

This becomes plain in two areas of his activity. Firstly, he did not regard the letter of the Law as the final arbiter of behaviour. Against the letter of the Law he healed on the Sabbath − several times, and quite deliberately.[9] Against the letter of the Law his disciples 'harvested' a few grains of wheat on the Sabbath, and failed to observe the strict rules about ritual washing before eating.[10] He expressed this principle of 'constructive disobedience' in a simple phrase: 'The sabbath was made for man, not man for the sabbath.'[11]

The second area, however, is even more distinctive. The Pharisees were particularly choosy about whom they ate with. 'Table fellowship' implied an acceptance of the other guests, and they felt that the principle of purity required them only to eat with Jewish men of recognised religious piety. Thus would the identity of the 'kingdom' be established. Every meal would be a foretaste of the promised messianic banquet when the faithful of Israel would sit down to eat in the court of their King: a vision they shared with the Essenes.

So again we can imagine the shock when Jesus chose, deliberately and as a matter of practice, to sit down at table with prostitutes and tax-collectors.[12] The prostitutes represented the very moral impurity which the Law condemned. They were, literally, 'outlaws', beyond the pale. But the tax-collectors were, if anything, even worse, for they were Jews who had accepted minor but profitable employment in the service of the usurping Romans. Their very income was tainted: it consisted of excess taxes charged over and above what the Romans required. They were traitors to Israel and consequently enemies of the kingdom of God.

So it is not surprising that the Pharisees were more baffled by Jesus' preference for the company of such people than by anything else that he did: 'This man welcomes sinners and eats with them!'

As with his attitude to the Romans, so here Jesus is demonstrating the fundamental difference between his message and that of those who came before. God's love is for *all*. He has no favourites. And the messianic message — and the banquet — is for sinners as well as (indeed, rather than) for the 'righteous': 'Those who are well do not need the physician, but those who are ill. I do not come to call the righteous, but sinners to repentance.'[13] His message was of course, directed at the 'lost sheep of the house of Israel', but the kingdom he spoke of knew no national or racial barriers.

So Jesus distanced himself from the Essenes and from the Pharisees in their narrow nationalism. What about the Zealots? It is, of course, a truism to say that he was against violence, and we have already considered his command to love our enemy. But, again, we shall not appreciate how shocking his 'pacifism' was unless we see it in its historical context.

The Zealots, after all, had a fair case. Rather like oppressed peoples today in Southern Africa or Latin America, they felt that all legitimate persuasion and appeals to reason had failed. It seemed that nothing could deliver them from the oppressor but their own hands and the shedding of their own blood, and that of their enemies. It must have looked as if Rome was an immovable, permanent and obdurate barrier to their free nationhood. If ever there was a case for a just war, for taking up arms to achieve liberty and justice, this was surely it.

It was an argument that appealed to many young Jews, especially in an area like Galilee. Surely if the whole nation rose up, and Jehovah was with them, even the legions of Rome could be thrown out and the throne of David restored? It was an attractive proposition, but an essential ingredient of success was that kind of implacable hatred of the enemy and ruthless determination which have always characterised effective popular revolutions.

Yet, faced with this, what did Jesus say? 'Do not resist an evil person. If someone strikes you on the right cheek, turn to him the other also . . . Blessed are the meek, for they will inherit the earth . . . blessed are the peacemakers, for they will be called sons of God.'[14] If the meek and the peace-

makers are to be blessed, then the Zealots were wrong to
stir up hatred and violence. If the people of Israel were to
turn the other cheek to their persecutors, then what would
become of the revolution? So, once again, Jesus set out the
difference: 'My kingdom is not of this world. If it were my
servants would *fight*'.[15] The message is different; the kingdom is different.

So the message of Jesus was new, even if the method by
which he put it across was traditional. Like many of the
religious teachers, the Scribes and Pharisees, Jesus used
parables — teaching stories — short epigrams and rhythmic
verses to convey his message. A good part of the teaching of
Jesus recorded in the Gospels, including the 'beatitudes' at
the start of the Sermon on the Mount, is in the form of
Hebrew poetry, parallelism — a feature which becomes
evident when they are translated back into the Aramaic in
which they were probably originally spoken:


> Ask and it will be given you;
> Seek and you will find;
> Knock and the door will be opened.
> For everyone who ask, receives;
> He who seeks, finds;
> And to him who knocks, the door will be opened.[16]


But despite the familiarity of the form, his teaching still
astonished the crowds: 'When Jesus had finished saying
these things, the crowds were amazed at his teaching,
because he taught as one who had authority, and not as
their teachers of the Law.'[17] In other words, the Jewish
teachers, the Scribes, merely interpreted a former revelation; Jesus offered a new one. The Scribes' authority was
the *Torah*, the Law of Jehovah; Jesus seemed to teach as
Jehovah's own spokesman. For a Jew, it was a staggering
assumption.

The gospel, or good news, of Jesus was centred, as we
have seen, on the idea of the kingdom of God, which was
now 'upon them'. As Don Cupitt has summarised it:

For those who had eyes to see, it was already apparent in the very activity of preaching it. It was a free gift, open to all, but an immediate response was necessary. It was no use being unprepared or making excuses, for there would be no second chance. The arrival of the kingdom overrode all other claims, so that for the sake of it one must be prepared to abandon work, money, family, home and even a sacred duty like burying the dead. In the new age which was arriving, human nature and the world itself would be transformed.[18]

We can see these ideas worked out in the famous parables of Jesus, those stories of universal appeal which illustrate from the life of field, farm and home the tremendous truths of the kingdom. Scholars have argued and fought over the Gospel texts in their attempts to decide which were, and which were not, the actual words and sayings of Jesus. All seem to agree that the parables are his, and reflect his message and his teaching style. So the people who declined the invitation to the wedding, and the foolish young women whose lamps ran out of oil as the bridegroom arrived, and the vineyard workers who rejected the owner's son and killed him, and the shepherd seeking the lost sheep rather than guarding the ones already in the fold all exemplify that startling message that the kingdom is here, that the priority is to accept God's gracious invitation and come into its ranks, and that *all* are to be pressed to enter, though, sadly, some will reject it.

What Jesus taught about himself is veiled, and apparently deliberately so. He never said, in so many words, 'I am the messiah', or 'I am the divine Son of God'. His preferred title for himself was 'the Son of Man', and whole books have been written on what he meant by that title. However, recent studies seem to suggest that earlier and extensive attempts to find the concept of the Son of Man in the Judaism of the time of Jesus are modern inventions.[19] The use of the title by Jesus was unusual, if not unique.

The origin of the phrase seems to have been a vision in the book of Daniel:

In my vision at night I looked, and there before me was one like a son of man, coming with the clouds of heaven. He approached the Ancient of Days and was led into his presence. He was given authority, glory and sovereign power; all peoples, nations and men of every language worshipped him. His dominion is an everlasting dominion that will not pass away, and his kingdom is one that will never be destroyed.[20]

Commentators and scholars seem to be agreed that the title 'son of man' in this passage is symbolical of Israel in triumph over the enemies who have been persecuting her. The 'son of man', in other words, is a symbol of the deliverance of God's people and the restoration of his kingdom.

That fits in well with the message of Jesus. The kingdom was upon them, and the Son of Man, himself, was the symbol and human representation of its presence. The moment of God's triumph had come, and was to be seen in what he, Jesus, said and did.

There are, of course, other elements in the teaching of Jesus in the Gospels, especially in his speeches about the future of Israel. Indeed, in the closing weeks of his life he seems to have concentrated on the coming time of testing and suffering, 'the birth-pangs of the new age', and upon his own role as the servant of God who must suffer and die to bring in the kingdom.

It seems to me impossible, in the light of all this, to argue, as some have done, that Jesus did not regard himself as the Messiah. All the main elements of his 'message', after applying the most scrupulous of critical tests to determine their authenticity, are messianic. If he did not consider himself to be the Messiah, then it is hard to imagine how he *did* see himself. To take the title 'Son of Man' would have been a mere affectation if he did not mean to imply that he was the holy one of God, the Saviour and bringer-in of the kingdom.

One final part of the teaching of Jesus must be mentioned before we go on to consider his actions, the things he did. Undoubtedly the best-known words of Jesus are the prayer which begins 'Our Father', and is often called the 'Lord's Prayer'. About its authenticity there is little doubt. James P. Mackey says, 'His prayer . . . is in a class apart as far as reliable authenticity is concerned.'[21] Indeed, its opening words in Latin, 'Pater noster', are to be found in a strange cryptogram unearthed in several ancient sites, most notably at Pompeii. That means – to the general amazement of the scholars – that the Lord's Prayer was known and used at Pompeii before AD 79, when the town was destroyed by the eruption of Vesuvius.

It is a prayer of such simplicity that a child can say it and understand every word, and yet of such complexity that no one really knows the full meaning of several phrases in it. What is beyond doubt is that it was, for Jesus, the kingdom-prayer, the prayer that was to be on the lips of those who responded to his urgent, instant invitation to 'repent and believe the good news'.

It was a prayer that emphasised, in a way that would have been startling to his hearers, the intimacy of God ('Our Father' – probably *abba* in Aramaic, or 'Dad'). It prayed for the coming of the kingdom on earth and defined it as the place where God's will was done, as it is perfectly in heaven. It made forgiveness the hallmark of the kingdom – God's forgiveness of us, and our consequent forgiveness of others (and not the other way round, as Matthew's version might be taken to imply). And, as the Essenes and Pharisees did, it saw purity and freedom from evil as the natural results of the reign of God in our lives and in society. No better summary exists of the 'message of Jesus' than these five short sentences. The 'shock of the new' that made his teaching so remarkable to his first hearers may not be so obvious to us today, but it is still there, for those who have eyes and imagination to see and feel it, even in these most familiar words of all.

# 8
## WHAT JESUS DID

One day, probably in Galilee, Jesus was faced with a man who was dumb. As usual, a crowd had gathered. The reputation of Jesus as a healer and exorcist, as well as a dynamic preacher, had gone ahead of him. He looked at the man, and, using a phrase that would have been familiar to the onlookers, he ordered the 'spirit of dumbness' to leave him. At once, the man began to speak.

So did some of the crowd, presumably Pharisees or other teachers of the Law.

'We know how he does this,' they said to anyone who would listen. 'He casts out evil spirits in the name of Beelzebub, the prince of the spirit-world. He's not a man of God, but an instrument of evil.'

And then some of them urged a test.

'How do we know you're from God? After all, Satan can do miracles, too. The only way for us to know whether you are working for God is if he gives us a sign from heaven, authenticating your work. Otherwise, we must assume you are an agent of the Adversary.'

'Any kingdom divided against itself is doomed,' Jesus replied. 'A divided household can't survive. So how will Satan survive if his kingdom is divided against itself, with some of his agents fighting against the others?

'Yet he *does* survive. So how can you say that I use that power of Beelzebub to drive out Beelzebub's own agents? It's nonsense.

'Not only that, but your followers also do exorcisms. In whose name do *they* do them? You don't accuse them of using the power of Beelzebub, do you?

'But look here. If I'm *not* using the power of Beelzebub, then the only other power with authority over the forces of evil is that of God. So if I'm driving out evil by the finger of God, then the kingdom of God really has come to you.'

Jesus turned his attention from his critics to hammer home his message to the crowd.

'Imagine a rich and powerful person with a house full of valuables. He makes it secure with locks and bolts and bars. He guards it with arms.

'The only way he can lose his wealth is if someone even more powerful comes along and over-powers him. When he has done that, he can strip the rich man of all his possessions.'

The bystanders knew exactly what he meant. They lived in a society which was deeply aware of the all-pervasive power of evil. Illness, paralysis, blindness, fits, deformity — all were seen as manifestations in God's world of the power of Satan, the 'Adversary'. To the devout Jew, there was no such thing as 'chance': the world was a battlefield in which a cosmic struggle was being waged between God and his Enemy. Indeed, to them it sometimes looked as though the Enemy had triumphed, though they were always careful to say that God would destroy him in the end.

So exorcisms were a comparatively common occurrence. The rabbis sometimes did them, and there is evidence that groups like the Essenes did, too. But here was Jesus marking his radical new teaching with the most dramatically effective exorcisms they had ever seen. As he said, there was only one possible explanation. Devil does not cast out devil, so, it must be that the power of God — 'the finger of God', in his own vivid phrase – was at work through Jesus. If that were so, two things followed. Jesus was the 'stronger man' of his parable, with power and authority to overcome Satan. And that meant that his whole ministry had God's authentication: 'The kingdom of God has come to you.'

It was, of course, a staggering claim to make, and a magnificent riposte to the envious criticisms of the Pharisees. He simply invited his hearers to look at the evidence. Did he, or did he not, look like the agent of God? Luke reports that following this altercation 'the crowds increased'[1], though Jesus had to warn them that they came for the wrong reason, 'asking for miraculous signs'. None would be given them, 'except the sign of Jonah' – the sign of

God's judgment warning people to repent before it is too late.

This one miracle — the healing of a dumb man — and the statement that followed it, may stand for the whole of Jesus' work of healing and exorcism. It is not so much that it is typical of his healings, but that it is exemplary. It is a rare instance of his doing something and then explaining its significance in totally unambiguous terms.

And there is little doubt of its authenticity. By every kind of test, this incident and conversation has the ring of truth. The accusation that Jesus cast out devils by the prince of devils has confirmation from secular history. The Jewish historian Josephus records similar accusations made about the healings performed by Jesus. The fact that his opponents were reduced to this kind of argument and exposed themselves to this kind of devastating riposte, is in itself strong evidence that Jesus performed many successful healings and exorcisms. Indeed, reports of such miracles are integral to all the most primitive records of his life. He was, quite simply, a preacher and healer. The two seem to be quite inseparable.

What was the nature of his healing? John Ferguson has described it like this:

It is clear that he had unusual gifts. Sometimes these were gifts of discernment; he was quick to get at the roots of illnesses which we would call psychosomatic. A good example is the account of the paralytic whose friends lowered him in a stretcher from a roof-top to bring him to Jesus. Jesus knew that his immobility arose from his sense of guilt, and declared the forgiveness of his sins; from this he was able to walk away, carrying his stretcher. But sometimes the healing seems to have been physical; it flowed through Jesus's fingers as the power of God at work in his world. Jesus, undemonstrative as he was about his healing work, saw his power in throwing down the demons of disease as evidence of God's present rule.[2]

There is no doubt that Jesus saw illness, disease and

deformity as evil things, contrary to the will of God. He was outraged by the sight of a man full of leprosy — he was 'moved with indignation'. Many afflictions are described in demonic terms — the dumb man had a 'spirit of dumbness', the woman bent double with some bone deformity had been 'bound by Satan for eighteen long years'.[3] The war against such afflictions was part of the more general war of God and his angels against the forces of disorder in the world.

Yet Jesus was quite clear that sickness was not necessarily the consequence of an individual's sin. That *was* a popular view at the time, and his disciples once asked him about the case of a man who had been blind from birth.

'Rabbi, who sinned, this man or his parents, that he was born blind?'

'Neither,' was the answer of Jesus. 'This happened so that the work of God might be displayed in his life'[4] — presumably, in the miracle of healing which followed. Again, it is assumed that there is no such thing as chance. Every facet of life is the direct consequence of the will of God or the baneful activities of his Adversary. But now, in Jesus, the power of God was at work in the world, and the most obvious demonstrations of it were the blind who could now see, the paralysed who could now walk, the dumb who could now speak.

Modern readers of the Gospels may well find this hard to take. I do not think many find the actual miracles to be incredible. There is a restraint and modesty about the way they occur and the way they are reported that makes them strangely convincing. But we find it hard to think of the world as a place where there is a constant and causal relationship between the will of God and every single event. For us, chance and accident are real words, with real meanings. For the first-century Jew they simply did not exist.

There is no logical reason to believe that our view of the world is better than theirs. Both depend upon a set of beliefs, a conditioning, which is part of our different world-views. But it is necessary to any intelligent reading of the

Gospels to allow for this all-pervasive cultural conditioning. They did not see the world through our eyes, and if we
wish to understand what they have written we must therefore try to see it through theirs.

It is not clear whether Jesus completely endorsed the
popular world-view of his time. There are hints, as we have
seen, that he did not: the blind man was not suffering as the
result of his own or his parents' sins, which would have been
the normal interpretation of his condition. Although Jesus
certainly cast out 'spirits', he also performed healings in
which there was no element of exorcism. Sometimes he
required an act of faith on the part of the sufferer; sometimes he did not. Sometimes, as we have seen, the forgiveness of sin was an integral part of the cure; more often, it
was not even mentioned.

It really seems to be wiser to accept the healing ministry
of Jesus as a fact, and not to try to build a doctrinal edifice
on top of it. Three things can be said about it, however.
First, Jesus clearly saw these healings as signs of the kingdom – manifestations of divine power that demonstrated its
arrival. God was at work, in a new and unique way, through
him.

Secondly, they were acts of love. These were not mere
demonstrations of naked power, done to astonish and
convince the onlookers or authenticate a message. They
were actions of 'compassion', expressions of a personal love
for individuals. Each miracle is a personal story rather than
a divine thunderbolt. There were tears and laughter involved: real people met a real man.

Thirdly, the miracles had an object which was over and
above the immediate healing of a single person's affliction.
Jesus saw his ministry of healing as part of a wider concern.
He had come to make men 'whole'. The obvious corollary
to that is that without healing they were somehow incom-
plete. For him, sickness, deformity, anxiety and sin were all
part of the same evil, the darkness that afflicts the whole
human race. He had come, the Son of Man, the divine
representative, to bring light, to dispel the darkness. His
ministry was indivisible. Wherever there was darkness, he

would shine the light of God. Wherever there were these evils which marred and defaced the image of God in his children, Jesus would overcome them and restore the image of his Father.

In a way, this was an image of the kingdom, too. The prophets of Israel had often depicted the troubles of the nation as a sickness, a wound, a terrible putrefying sore in the body. And they had always seen the coming of the golden age, the kingdom, as marked by the healing of those deep-seated wounds.

So now, with the arrival of Jesus, the sudden spate of healings was a sign which people could recognise: 'The kingdom of God has come to you.' Every wretched blind beggar who had his sight restored, every cripple who could throw away his crutches, every tortured epileptic or schizophrenic released from the mental darkness of his condition, was a visible fulfilment of the prophecy of Isaiah with which Jesus had begun his public ministry in the synagogue at Nazareth:

> The Spirit of the Lord is upon me,
> because he has anointed me
> to preach good news to the poor.
> He has sent me to proclaim freedom
> for the prisoners
> and recovery of sight for the blind,
> to release the oppressed,
> to proclaim the year of the Lord's favour.[5]

So the miracles of healing which were undoubtedly part of the ministry of the Jesus of history supplement and confirm his spoken message. But does that apply to the handful of other miracles, the three or four occasions when Jesus is recorded as doing something miraculous that was not a healing or exorcism? I am thinking of the feeding of the five thousand, the walking on the water and the calming of the storm. These miracles clearly fall into a different category altogether. Many people who would have little difficulty in accepting that Jesus had a most remarkable power of healing would gib at the idea that he could walk on the surface of a lake or command a violent storm to be still.

The usual explanation for the presence of these miracles in the Gospel records is that they are the mythical accretions that grow up around any cult figure in religious history. Pious sermon illustrations are taken literally, and soon pass into the historical records. So it is but a step, the argument goes, from saying that 'Jesus calms the storm in your heart, just like the calm after a great storm', to the creation of a story enshrining that idea, of Jesus actually calming a real, meteorological storm and at the same time quietening the fears of his disciples.

So the argument goes, and from the point of view of the historical scholar it is fairly convincing. Although, as we shall see later, I do not entirely accept it, I could not argue that these phenomenal miracles should be included in a synopsis of those things in the life of Jesus which can be regarded as historically authenticated. They may have happened; I may believe them to have happened. But they do not have the weight of evidence behind them that the healing miracles and exorcisms do.

What were the other things that Jesus did, the typical actions that marked out his personality and his intentions? We have considered some already, in his somewhat cavalier treatment of the Sabbath, and his willingness to go outside his stated ministry to 'the lost sheep of the house of Israel' to help a Syro-Phoenician woman, a Samaritan and even a Roman centurion.

We have also mentioned his habit of eating and drinking with the moral outcasts of Jewish society, the tax-collectors and prostitutes. We should simply add at this stage that meals figured prominently in his life and work. The ritual meal was a feature of the religious sects of the time. It symbolised their unity. It excluded strangers and aliens. It looked ahead to the great victory banquet of the kingdom.

For most of the time Jesus seemed to be using the meal for quite different ends. He chose to eat with outcasts, when the very best religious tables were open to him. 'Today,' he told the swindler Zacchaeus, 'today I must eat at your house.'[6] And he did not deny the charge levelled by the Pharisees that he made a habit of eating with prostitutes and other notorious sinners.

Jesus seemed to be deliberately reversing the contemporary attitude to table fellowship. 'They' saw the table as exclusive to the chosen people, cleansed, purified and law-abiding. *He* saw it as an open table, where the beggars, the cripples, the outcasts and the morally disabled were actually more welcome than the conventionally, 'righteous'.[7] His disciples did not observe the strict rites of cleansing before eating their meals.[8] He and his followers were not teetotallers, like John and his disciples, nor ascetic and self-denying, like the Essenes and some of the other strict sects. They were known as good eaters and good drinkers.[9] The hallmark of the fellowship which formed around Jesus seems to have been a kind of relaxed joy which was totally foreign to the Judaism of the time, and a happy meal together seems to have been the keynote of it.

So it is not surprising that the only ritual action of Jesus to have been preserved throughout the two-thousand-year history of the Christian Church is a meal, the so-called 'Last Supper'. On the night of his betrayal, almost certainly at the Passover 'seder', Jesus sat down to a meal with the twelve, his chosen 'apostles'. After supper, he took the cup of wine and invited them all to share it with him. The gesture was familiar, but the words with which he introduced it were strange enough to make a lasting impression, so that they are recorded in Matthew, Mark and Luke, and, in an even earlier manuscript, by Paul, in almost identical terms: 'This cup is the new covenant in my blood. Do this, whenever you drink it, in remembrance of me.' Similarly he broke the bread – presumably the unleavened bread of the Passover – and passed it to them: 'This is my body, which is for you; do this in remembrance of me.'

It was as if all the meals that Jesus had enjoyed with them were meant to lead up to this. To eat with someone, to 'break bread' with them, was tantamount, in the ancient world, to making a covenant of fellowship with them. You could not betray a person with whom you had enjoyed table fellowship. (It was this that seems to have incensed the Gospel writers most about the treachery of Judas Iscariot.) But Jesus was going beyond this. He was speaking of his 'body' and 'blood' as inaugurating a new covenant, of which they were the first recipients, and this meal, celebrated by them after his departure, would be the sign and seal of it.

The idea of the 'new covenant' would have been familiar to the disciples. The 'old covenant' was the one God made with Israel through Moses, which was commemorated in the Passover meal, the 'seder'. If they kept the Law, he would be their God, and they would be his people.

But from Jeremiah onwards the idea had gained ground that there would one day be a 'new' covenant, of a far more profound kind, to replace the old one, which had manifestly failed − not on God's side, but on theirs, because they had not kept the Law.

'The time is coming,' declares the Lord, 'When I will make a new covenant with the house of Israel and with the house of Judah. It will not be like the covenant I made with their forefathers when I took them by the hand to lead them out of Egypt, because they broke my covenant, though I was a husband to them,' declares the Lord. 'This is the covenant that I will make with the house of Israel after that time,' declares the Lord. 'I will put my law in their minds and write it on their hearts. I will be their God, and they will be my people. No longer will a man teach his neighbour, or a man his brother, saying,"Know the Lord," because they will all know me, from the least of them to the greatest', declares the Lord. 'For I will forgive their wickedness, and will remember their sins no more.'[10]

The mention of a 'new covenant' by Jesus must have recalled this passage to his hearers. The day had come! The old agreement, based on external observation of the letter of the Law, was to be superseded by a new one. This new agreement would have three elements in it that were miss-

ing from the old one. The 'Law' would be put into their
hearts — presumably meaning that it would be a matter of
inner conviction rather than external persuasion. Everyone, from highest to lowest, would 'know the Lord' — a
more intimate, personal religion than formerly. And the
covenant would include an irrevocable commitment by
God to the forgiveness of their sins, not ritually or temporarily, but really and permanently.

For Jesus, this 'last supper', which has become the
'Lord's Supper', or the eucharist, was the sign of the new
covenant. Again, it was a staggering claim to make – that his
body and blood, to be offered for the kingdom, were the
marks of the long-promised new agreement with God,
superseding the one made with Moses. It is hard to believe
that he did not see this as a messianic action; and certainly
his followers then, in the immediate future and in the long
sweep of history, have all seen it as an event invested with
the most enormous spiritual significance, all the more so, of
course, as it coincided with the Passover, the great remembrance of God's deliverance of Israel from slavery in Egypt.

So we have the ministry of Jesus marked by message,
miracle and meal, all pointing to the same conclusion:
something new and unique was happening, events were at a
turning point in history, and things could never be the same
again. As God had delivered the people of the old covenant
from Egypt and brought them to a promised land under
Moses, so he was to deliver his people of the new covenant
from their slavery to sin and bring them into his promised
kingdom. It would be a greater and more far-reaching
deliverance, and would require a greater deliverer than
Moses. It is a measure of his confidence in his own destiny
that Jesus could see himself as precisely that deliverer.

# 9

# WHAT WAS JESUS LIKE?

It is difficult – if not impossible – to establish with any degree of certainty what Jesus looked like. Strangely, in view of the full and detailed accounts of his death and the fairly lengthy reporting of his public utterances, no one seems to have considered it important to tell us what he looked like. Or, if they did, we have lost it.

One theory suggests that the only description of Jesus's appearance written by a contemporary was so unflattering that the Christians of the post-apostolic era could not take it, and deliberately 'lost' it. Certainly echoes of a description occur in secondary sources in the first three centuries, and they suggest that he was short, physically weak and even unprepossessing. For those brought up on the handsome, flaxen-haired giant of the illustrated children's Bible, such a description may come as a rude shock, even if it is in line with the prophecy in Isaiah of Jehovah's suffering Servant, 'He has nothing about his appearance that is attractive.'[1]

It is more likely that those who recorded the life of Jesus either regarded a physical description of him as irrelevant to their task, or simply had nothing on which to base it. Mark probably saw Jesus, but he was a teenager at the time; the final compilers of the other Gospels probably had access to the memoirs of people who met Jesus personally, but had never seen him themselves. They worked, as we have seen, from collections of his sayings and semi-credal statements about his death and resurrection. There was little here on which to build a description of him, though plenty to suggest that he was *not* physically weak. He seems to have made a practice of rising early, of missing sleep altogether at times, and of walking great distances – for instance, from Tyre across Lebanon to Galilee, by way of Caesarea Philippi, some sixty of the hottest miles in the

Near East. And there is no hint of his ever being unwell.

On the other hand, the Gospel writers do present us with enough material to answer the question, 'What was Jesus like?' in the sense of 'What sort of a person was he?' And it is remarkably consistent, considering the different sources on which they drew.

For instance, the first three Gospels give us a very good idea of the speech mannerisms and style of Jesus. As we have seen, he used sayings, rhythmic speech, stories and parables. But it is what he said, and how he said it, that reveals something of his personality.

Jesus was an acute observer of human behaviour. Very often an apparently dry, didactic story is lit up by some penetrating insight. Luke's account of the parable of the Prodigal Son is a splendid example.[2]

Simply to convey the point he was making, Jesus need have said no more than that there were two sons, the elder one loyal and hard-working on his father's estate, the younger one a wastrel who squandered his money in the far city; but that when the wastrel saw his own folly, and made for home, he was welcomed back by his father, despite the objections of the good son, who felt affronted that his father still treated them both as equally precious. The point is much the same as in the parable of the lost sheep: 'I did not come to call the righteous, but sinners to repentance.'

But in fact the story is tricked out with brilliant little flashes of observation. The younger son, starving in the city, gets a job feeding pigs (which would have made him virtually a heathen, in the eyes of orthodox Judaism), and would cheerfully have eaten the pigs' food, had he been allowed. After his return, when father has put the best robe on him, had the fatted calf killed, and ordered the welcome-home party to begin, the elder brother, out in the fields (a nice touch!), hears the sound of music and revelry. He is understandably aggrieved. He had never been given a party, or a robe, or a fatted calf to eat with his friends, or even, as he says, 'a mere kid', yet when this profligate returns, 'who has squandered your money on prostitutes', he is welcomed back with open arms and given a hero's reception. The whole conversation is a fascinating piece of imaginative dialogue. If it were all we had of the stories of Jesus, we should know without doubt that he was a story-teller of the first rank.

As usual with Jesus, irony is frequently just below the surface. He seems to have enjoyed the fascinating discrepancies between how people see themselves, and how other people see them. The older son saw himself as justifiably aggrieved, righteously indignant that his father was being shamelessly manipulated by his irresponsible younger brother. Probably Jesus's audience felt the same, and he enjoyed leading them on to the final words of the father, which indicate that the rejoicing over the prodigal's return is entirely justified and proper. Perhaps some of them caught the full irony of it: Israel is the prodigal; its self-appointed moral arbiters, the scribes and Pharisees, are the elder son. And the party, I suppose, is the kingdom of God.

A similar if broader irony is in the sketch of the two men, one with a plank in his eye, the other with a speck of dirt in it. 'Let me help you remove your speck', says the man with the plank − and takes his place for all time with those maddening people who are hawk-eyed about the faults of others, and totally blind to their own.

Jesus used language pungently, which suggests that he was far from being 'meek and mild', as the children's hymn describes him. A man who could call the religious teachers of his day 'white-washed sepulchres', 'blind leaders of the blind', 'play-actors' who practise fraud on helpless widows 'and for a pretence make long prayers', is both brave and forthright. There is a sharp edge to the words of Jesus, and quite a few people cut themselves on it.

It may well be that other sayings of Jesus which we find hard to understand were examples of irony which his hearers, or at any rate some of them, would have understood perfectly. His apparent commendation of the steward who dishonestly ingratiated himself with his master's debtors is almost certainly to be understood as irony.[3] So may be his answer to the rather ingenuous offer of his disciples to take two swords with them to the garden of Gethsemane on the night of his betrayal.

'That's enough,' he said.

It is hard to imagine that the man who said 'those who take the sword, die by the sword' could have been endorsing the carrying of weapons — it is in flat contradiction of almost everything we know of Jesus. But it is possible, in view of the likely nature and size of the arresting force, that the laconic comment of Jesus that two swords would be 'enough' meant that two swords would be as effective as none, or for that matter twenty. The Temple guards, and behind them the Roman legions, were not going to be thwarted by a couple of swords in the hands of a dozen rustics from Galilee.

There are so many similar instances in the recorded speeches and conversations of Jesus that it is astonishing to find one distinguished author of an earlier generation, whose book about Jesus was held in great respect by many devout Christians, could actually write this: 'Irony is unthinkable in connection with Jesus, for his feeling of power made it unnecessary. Those who believe they can find it in his utterances are putting their own meaning into his words.'[4]

It is notoriously difficult to be dogmatic about figures of speech, but if Jesus did not use irony then one is at a loss to know who ever has.

What could it be but irony when Jesus accused the Pharisees, in their zeal for observing the minute details of the Law while evading its weightier demands, of 'straining out a gnat and swallowing a camel'? Or when he asked the crowds who went out to the desert to see John the Baptist whether they expected to see him dressed in fine clothes — 'those who wear expensive clothes and indulge in luxury are in palaces': not deserts, and not wearing a camel's hair loin-cloth! Or, indeed, when he congratulated the Samaritan woman on telling the truth when she said she had no husband: 'The fact is, you have had five husbands, and the man you now have is not your husband. What you have just said is quite true!'[5]

Irony also lends colour and bite to many sayings that are otherwise unremarkable. Setting his face for Jerusalem, Jesus is warned by some friendly Pharisees to go somewhere else, as Herod intends to kill him. His reply is fascinating: 'Surely no prophet can die outside Jerusalem!'

Literally it is meaningless — prophets had died in all sorts of places. But as an example of irony it is devastating. Jerusalem, the holy city, the city of David, crammed to its walls with priests and rabbis and scribes, stuffed full of holy monuments and the location of the very Temple of God — where else could a prophet be so sure to be rejected!

But the irony was not unkind or destructive. In this case for instance, Jesus went immediately into his most moving lament over Jerusalem: 'O Jerusalem, Jerusalem, you who kill the prophets and stone those sent to you, how often have I longed to gather your children together, as a hen gathers her chicks under her wings, but you were not willing!'[6]

It is equally surprising that Dr Otto Borchert, in the book just quoted, should assert quite categorically that humour had no appeal for Jesus: 'Fun and humour found no place in Jesus' life, because the strain induced by the sin of the world was too great. He lacked that smiling ease without which humour is impossible. Did he ever actually laugh?'[7]

Now it is true that we are not told that Jesus laughed, and we have no certain record of any 'jokes' from his lips. That is not surprising. Only twice in the entire Bible is an instance of somebody laughing reported as a matter of factual description — and both of those are in Genesis. We are not told that St Paul laughed, or St Peter, or the Virgin Mary, or Moses, or King David or Solomon. It seems a strange deduction to assume that not one of these people ever laughed, or had a place for fun and humour in their lives, simply because we are never told of specific instances. Arguments from silence are rarely convincing.

However, in the case of Jesus, as we have seen, humour certainly did have a place in his speech. The story of the plank and the speck in the eye would surely have made its hearers laugh. Did Jesus keep a straight face? It seems unlikely that Jesus would have had the affection of children if he had been totally without fun, or have retained the loyalty of his close associates for so long without a sense of humour.

It is, however, typical of any attempt to assess the character of Jesus that there appears to be an elusive quality which underlies all we know about him. Constantly, both in reading the New Testament and also other people's assessment of it, one is aware that in Jesus high seriousness, of a quite uncommon degree of intensity, co-existed with an infectious sense of joy. He could utter words of quite devastating warning, and yet his reputation was of someone who lacked the gravity and sobriety of John or the Pharisees. He was told to curb his followers' exuberance, but replied that they were like revellers at a wedding party. Time enough, he said, for the high seriousness later on. His progress through Galilee was clearly marked by joy, and his entry into Jerusalem, riding on an ass, was more like a carnival than anything else.

What Jesus seemed to give to people was the joy of innocence. He had only scorn for those who lived in palaces and found their pleasures in self-indulgence, but he called his followers to a party, not a wake. He was aware of, and especially in the closing weeks of his life frequently spoke about, the dark side of events. His was not the kind of fun that ignores reality. He wept at the tomb of a friend, and he wept over the folly and blindness of Jerusalem. But joy – an innocent enjoyment of the Father's world – was the hallmark of his followers, and they retained it after he had left them. It is simply impossible to imagine that Jesus and the twelve disciples of his choice never had a good laugh together.

It is said you can tell a person by the company he keeps. It is also true that you can judge a person's character by the loyalty he evokes in others. In Jesus's case the two tests again produce a kind of contradiction. Jesus did not seek the company of the good and great. Indeed, there is very little remarkable about his choice of close friends – the twelve disciples – except how unremarkable they were:

simply a typical dozen young Galilean men of the time, with a slight bias, if anything, towards the unconventional. They included, on the evidence of the Gospels, some who were motivated by the worst kind of ambition – to attain power over others;[8] some who had a nasty streak of violence in them;[9] a former crooked tax-collector, an ex-terrorist and a bombastic braggart who was totally blind to his own short-comings.[10] And, of course, there was one who was a traitor.

These assessments can be regarded as authentic, for the early Church was hardly likely to publish defamatory statements about its founding fathers, the apostles (as they were later known), unless they were demonstrably and unavoidably true.

Apart from these close companions, whom he welded eventually into an effective leadership team, Jesus habitually kept company with the outcasts of society, as we have seen. If history had judged Jesus by the company he kept, he would not have been regarded as a great moral and religious leader.

Yet if he were to be judged by the loyalty of his friends, and their devotion to him, the result would be quite different. It is true that his male followers temporarily deserted him at the time of his arrest, but such was the hold he had on them that they gathered together after his death, almost as though they could not bear to accept that he had left them. But throughout his ministry, and, of course, especially after they were convinced of his resurrection, the 'eleven' were prepared to face ridicule, deprivation, poverty and mis-understanding, and eventually, almost all of them, violent death, out of loyalty to Jesus.

The male disciples, then, had a good record of loyalty. But the female disciples had an even better one. And the reason is simple. No male had ever treated women as Jesus did. Again we may safely conclude that we are on sound historical ground, for no writer of the age could possibly have invented as revolutionary an approach to women as Jesus had, according to the Gospels. It is not surprising that their response to it was an astonishing loyalty. When the male disciples fled, at the time of the arrest, the women followed him into the city, hung around the court and then waited by his cross. The women guarded his broken body, wrapped it in its shroud, and came on the Sunday morning ready to perform the last service of embalming it.

In the Israel of Bible times, as in the ancient world generally, women were regarded as inferior to men. The husband was the head of the household and his wife or wives were under his absolute authority. The female role was more or less restricted to child-bearing, child-rearing and domestic duties. Where religion was concerned, women were kept apart from men in the Jewish synagogue and were not allowed to approach the altar in the Temple. Divorce was easy for the man but impossible for the wife. It is not surprising that the Jewish prayers to this day include a (male) thanksgiving, 'I thank thee that I am not a woman'.

This notion of female inferiority was general in the ancient world, as we have seen, but in no period was the inferiority so emphasised as in the rabbinical Judaism of New Testament times. The rules and traditions were restrictive enough, but they were matched in practice by a kind of male chauvinism unimaginable in the modern world. In matters of public concern, it was assumed that only men would participate. Speeches were addressed to the 'men of Israel'. Wives were simply assumed to go along with male decisions on everything. The opinion of a woman would not be sought and if it were offered it would be disregarded. As she became her husband's property on marriage, all her possessions also automatically became his, which made her dependent upon him absolutely and removed any notion of independent thought or action.

So far as anyone can tell, Jesus was the first man in the history of Israel, and possibly of the ancient world, to ignore this assumed inferiority of women. There is plenty of evidence that he treated them in exactly the same way as he treated man − and often shocked his (male) disciples by doing so. On one occasion he went out of his way to sit by a well and talk at length with an immoral Samaritan woman.[11] It would have been surprising for any male Jew to sit and converse with a Samaritan of any kind − they were regarded as religiously corrupt. It would have been even more surprising if the Samaritan were a woman. Yet more surprising to talk to her *alone*. And totally unthinkable if she were also notoriously promiscuous.

Yet Jesus did exactly that. He risked offending the men and alienating the crowds by spending time on his own with someone who needed it. And his conversation with her was not about trivia. It concerned morality, and worship, and the Messiah: not usually considered to be matters of womanly concern at that time.

This was not even an isolated incident. Jesus obviously spent a great deal of time talking about the deepest spiritual concerns with Mary of Bethany[12] – somewhat to her sister Martha's disapproval. Another Mary, of Magdala, had a depth of devotion to him that could only have arisen from the most profound sense of indebtedness. Jesus cared about the despised prostitutes on the streets, the despised Syro-Phoenician Gentile woman,[13] and the desperate woman in Galilee who had had what the King James Version delicately calls 'an issue of blood' – in medical terms, menorrhagia – for twelve years.[14]

This last case is particularly interesting. Under Jewish Law, a woman in menstruation was 'unclean', and anyone who touched her was also considered 'unclean'.[15] Yet this woman pushed through the crowd in order to touch Jesus's garment in search of healing for her illness. She was desperate. She had 'spent her entire living on doctors' in search of a cure, and they had not been able to help. But Jesus could, and did. He stopped in the crowd and singled her out. She stood in front of him in 'fear and trembling' – as well she might, having made him, a 'rabbi' in the people's eyes, unclean by touching him. Yet Jesus had no condemnation for her at all.

'Daughter,' he said – the only time he is recorded as using this form of address, a particularly intimate and reassuring one – 'Daughter, enter into peace. Your faith has healed you.' And so once again tradition was flouted, or rather, totally ignored. There is no word about uncleanness; just love, sympathy and understanding of her despair. And a studied disregard for traditions and laws that made women inferior, or unclean, *simply because they were women*.

There was another down-trodden group in the ancient world to whom Jesus especially addressed himself, the poor. The prophets of the Old Testament, of course, had frequently taken up the cause of the poor, and denounced those who exploited and suppressed them. And charity towards the poor was a prominent feature of the Law of Israel.

But Jesus identified with the poor in a new way. He came from a poor home, he lived a life of impecunious simplicity ('the Son of Man has nowhere to lay his head') and he clearly felt more 'at home' with those who had nothing than with those who had everything.

As we have seen already, he announced his ministry in startling terms, reading out in the synagogue at Nazareth a prophecy of Isaiah about the coming servant of Jehovah:

> The Spirit of the Lord is upon me,
>   because he has anointed me to preach.
> He has sent me to proclaim
>   freedom for the prisoners
>   and recovery of sight for the blind,
> to release the oppressed,
>   to proclaim the year of the Lord's favour.

He then 'rolled up the scroll, gave it back to the attendant and sat down. The eyes of everyone in the synagogue were fastened on him, and he said to them, "Today this scripture is fulfilled in your hearing".'

It was an astonishing claim with which to launch his ministry, and led within a few minutes to a crowd who had until then been impressed with the 'gracious words' which had come from the lips of a local man becoming incensed at his arrogance and eventually driving him out of the town and attempting to throw him down a cliff.

They were not at this point rejecting his implied claim to be the Messiah, but his refusal to give special status to his home town and district, or even to the people of Israel. He had pointed out instances in the Old Testament where prophets healed and worked miracles for Gentiles and foreigners rather than for their own kith and kin.

Yet in rejecting him they were ignoring the point at which he had offered to begin this prophetic ministry — 'to preach good news to the *poor*'. Most of them were poor, some of them very poor, and few, if any of them were rich. Had they been able to see it, he was identifying with them in their powerlessness and poverty, rather than in their race and religion; and this became a distinctive mark of his progress through Galilee and beyond.

Unlike the Old Testament prophets, Jesus did not take up the 'cause' of the poor. Indeed, in one respect he regarded them as advantaged: 'Blessed are you who are poor', he assured his disciples, 'for yours is the kingdom of God.'[16] Without the crippling handicap of wealth, they could address themselves to things that really mattered: 'How hard it is for the rich to enter the kingdom of God! Indeed, it is easier for a camel to go through the eye of a needle than for a rich man to enter the kingdom of God.'[17]

In parable and preaching he expanded on this apparently grim saying. The rich fool[18] went about his business, expanding his interests, building up wealth, until the night when God demanded his life, and all he had worked for went to someone else. 'This is how it will be,' commented Jesus, 'with anyone who stores up things for himself but is not rich towards God.' The beggar Lazarus longed to eat the scraps that fell from a rich man's table. Yet when they both died, the rich man ('who was dressed in purple and fine linen and lived in luxury every day') went to torment, and Lazarus ('covered with sores') went to Abraham's side.[19]

Wealth, in the teaching of Jesus, is a distraction. Possessions are tawdry toys, soon consumed by moth or rust, of no significance or value in the light of eternity. We would be better off without them.

But it would be a travesty of his teaching to suggest that this was no more than a 'pie in the sky when you die' philosophy. Jesus was not indifferent to the appalling inequalities and injustices of the society in which he lived, as the story of the rich man and Lazarus indicates. He did not simply accept that the poor should go hungry, or the rich wallow in their luxury.

The revolution he urged, however, was not the overthrow of the social order but the transformation of the human heart. He undermined the established framework by showing people a completely different set of values, which would inevitably lead to a completely different way of living. I think it is fair to say that history has vindicated his approach, though sometimes there has been a long time-lag between the transformation of the heart and the transformation of society. It took eighteen centuries of Christianity for Christians to accept that slavery was incompatible with the Gospel. And other evils – social distinctions, racial prejudice, exploitation of the weak – have still not surrendered to the mental revolution he began. Yet the changes in moral and social attitudes since the coming of the Christian era are so marked, and contrast so sharply with those in parts of the world that have not had this long Christian influence, that it seems only fair to give Jesus the credit for them.

Yet in one sense even that inner transformation was not the central element, the primary concern, of the teaching of Jesus. The part of his message that had the most astounding newness, and, one guesses, attracted people more than anything else, was about forgiveness – our forgiveness of others, and God's forgiveness of us.

For Jesus, this was a matter of *acceptance*. We accept those who wrong us because, decisively, *God accepts us*. Like the father of the prodigal, watching the road and waiting to welcome with open arms his foolish and wayward son, God actually seeks us out. He is not, as most of the religions of the time of Jesus saw him, a remote, cold, demanding Judge, but a loving, forgiving Father.

'Lord,' Peter asked Jesus on one occasion, 'How often should I forgive my brother when he sins against me? Seven times?'

Peter clearly thought he had pitched his offer on the

generous side. After all, to be deliberately wronged seven times by the same person would try the forbearance of most of us. But the answer of Jesus was on a different plane altogether.

'No,' he said, 'until seventy times seven.'

With seven the 'perfect' number for the Jews – the figure of completeness – the answer was simply a way of saying, 'without end'. And for Jesus that was not a matter of being generous, kind or broadminded about sin, but of reflecting the character of God, his 'heavenly Father'.

God *accepts* us; we accept each other. Right at the heart of the life of Jesus, as well as his teaching, was this concept of acceptance. As John puts it in the fourth Gospel, 'God did not send his Son into the world to condemn the world, but that the world might be saved through him.'[20] Jesus went about accepting people, including many who were rejected by just about everyone else: the 'leper', the harlot, the renegade, the cheat, the beggar, the outcast, the pauper. By that acceptance he was not condoning anything they had done that was morally wrong; he was making it clear that nothing they had done had cut them off from the love of God. All are welcome in the Father's kingdom, but especially those who had previously rejected it. All the sheep are at home in the Shepherd's fold, but especially the one that had been lost.

It was not a totally new concept – the Old Testament often speaks of God's patient love and forgiveness – but it was applied in a daringly new way. For Jesus, forgiveness was the key that could break the moral log-jam of history. Law, ritual, penalties, judgment had failed to break down barriers, heal wounds or bring peace of mind. But in what he said and what he did – most tellingly in his death – Jesus argued and demonstrated a different way: not so much rejecting evil as accepting it, taking it into himself, opening himself to the wounds and sorrows of others; and yet still clearly and unambiguously against all that is evil.

One incident recorded in the synoptic Gospels may serve to illustrate how he dealt with evil.[21] A man 'full of leprosy' came to him. 'Leprosy' in the Bible is not the disease called by that name today. It seems to have been a serious and contagious skin disease, which was widely feared and led to the sufferers being compulsorily isolated from society. They often lived in caves or little clusters of hovels away from the towns and villages, and when 'normal' people approached them, they were required to ring a warning bell or shout out, 'Unclean, unclean!'

Since Old Testament times, 'leprosy' had been a common picture or analogy of sin. It was seen as something that had taken root in human nature, that spread irresistibly, and that cut off the sufferer, the sinner, from God. Sin is uncleanness; sin is contagious; and sin isolates.

There was little doubt, then, when Jesus was confronted by this man 'full of leprosy', that the watchers at the time, and the reporters later, would have seen it as a confrontation between the power and purity of God and the darkness and corruption of evil. That may be nonsense medically, but it is a fact historically. So several things in the biblical descriptions of what followed are highly relevant to our understanding of Jesus's view of sin and cleansing from sin.

In the first place, when Jesus saw the man who was 'full of leprosy' he was 'moved with compassion' or even, as some translators argue, 'moved with indignation'. Both translations suggest that the sight of the leprosy affected him deeply − to compassion, sympathy for the man's plight; or indignation, anger at the evil thing that had caused it. In either case, the strong suggestion is that Jesus found the man's illness in some way offensive − it was against nature, against the will of his Father. Indeed, his whole healing ministry could be interpreted in terms of a protracted war against a malign power that had somehow infiltrated the creation.

The man asked for healing in words that suggest an act of faith: 'If you will, you can cleanse me.' He wanted to be rid of the disease (which was hardly surprising) and he believed that Jesus could do it (which was).

Then Jesus 'stretched out his hand and touched him', saying, 'I will. Be clean.'

The gesture of touching the leper is in itself important. Presumably it was not necessary to the healing – Jesus healed others without touching them – but it was highly significant in the case of a leper. Because the disease was considered to be contagious, no one touched lepers. Indeed, as we have seen, they were required to live away from other people, in caves and leper camps, so that every kind of contact was kept to a minimum. Yet Jesus quite deliberately touched him, a gesture of friendship and acceptance, as well as healing. And in accepting the leper, Jesus cured him.

Now there can be no doubt that Jesus hated leprosy and all that it had done to human beings. But he was able to distinguish between the disease and the sufferer. He was able to accept the leper but reject the disease. And when he did, the whole situation was transformed.

I do not think it is at all fanciful, or going beyond what the contemporary records intended to convey, to contrast the traditional attitude towards leprosy (and, by analogy, sin) with that of Jesus. The normal approach was to isolate the sufferer, to cut him off from the community, and to ensure that he did not contaminate others. That is not an unfair picture of the Pharisaic attitude to sin. Let the sinner be kept at a distance, far from the 'good' people who might be harmed by him.

But the approach of Jesus was radically different. He accepted the sufferer, 'risked' contamination, healed him and then restored him to the community. He was prepared to expose himself, and others, to contamination rather than leave one poor soul cut off from the kingdom. His whole ministry, as we have seen, was geared towards the outcast, the outsider, the 'lost sheep'. All were welcome, provided they wished to be rid of their disease, their sin; and provided they turned to Jesus for help.

So we can visualise the ministry of Jesus. It lasted between two and three years – the mere flicker of a candle in the darkness of history. It was confined to a small area about the size of Wales, and within that it was almost entirely restricted to one people, the Jews. It consisted of preaching, largely through parables and sayings, miracles and exorcisms. It attracted a fairly large following, but the people who responded to it were mostly from the powerless part of society, and most of them fell away when it became clear that Jesus was heading for a confrontation with the Jewish as well as the Roman authorities, and that he had no political ambitions whatever. It was a ministry to *Israel*, which seems to have avoided even the hellenised, Greek-speaking, less devout towns and villages of Galilee. But it was above all a ministry to the 'lost sheep' of Israel, to those who knew they were poor and powerless but responded to a message of love and acceptance. No wonder it was recorded that 'the common (i.e. the poor) people heard him gladly'.[22]

One thing remains to be said in this attempted picture of what Jesus was 'like'. He was a man of action, and in this he was different from most of the great religious figures of history. Those brief years were packed with event. Even the incidents we have in the Gospels would have kept a healthy man busy over such a period of time, and we are told that they are by no means an exhaustive list of everything he said and did.[23] Yet he retained a calm and a serenity. The breathless record of Mark's Gospel, where the most common adverb is 'immediately', still gives us a picture of a man who had time to meditate and pray, who had time for people and for his friends, and who was never rushed or pressurised.

A colleague of mine, John Newbury, sat in a Hindu Ashram, of the Raja Yogi sect, in India, and read the opening section of Mark's Gospel. This is how he described its impact on him in a subsequent broadcast:

As I read, I was astounded at how Jesus came across to me. Yes, he did meditate. Yes, he did detach himself from the world. Yes, he was pure. But Mark's Gospel is packed full of action. Jesus *does things*. He convinces friends to follow him, he astounds people by his teaching, he casts out demons, he cures fevers, fetishes and foolishness. He prays, he preaches, he meets the outcasts, he claims them as special people. He overturns the accepted order of things. And that's just chapter one!

Earlier we commented how Jesus seemed to combine high seriousness with an infectious sense of joy. Now we find a life of intense activity combined with a sense of detachment, of serenity. We could equally well say that Jesus combined an almost ruthless rejection of sin with an apparently unbounded acceptance of the sinner.

These paradoxes are not 'problems' in assessing what Jesus was like. They *are* what he was like. There emerges from the Gospels the picture of a man who was at once so complex and so single-minded, so serious and yet so joyful, so calm and yet so active, that his character could not have been invented. He was 'like' no one who had gone before. No one who has lived since has shown the same breadth of character. He was unique in his time, and it is at least arguable that he is unique in all the history of our race. At any rate we may safely say that Jesus of Nazareth is one of the most 'unusual' people who have ever lived.

# 10

# THE LAST WEEK

The last week of the life of Jesus is a study in contrasts. He entered Jerusalem to a hero's welcome on the Sunday. On the Friday he was dying the death of a common criminal, hanging from a Roman cross overlooking the road on the other side of the city.

It was not the first visit Jesus had paid to Jerusalem. Every devout Jew was expected to go up to the city at least once a year, for Passover − preferably three times, to include other great festivals. Luke tells us of a visit Jesus made when he was a boy, and the fourth Gospel refers to several visits he made to Jerusalem during the period of his ministry.

But there is little doubt that this last journey to Jerusalem was different, both for Jesus and his followers. He 'set his face to go up to Jerusalem'. Despite warnings that arrest and perhaps execution awaited him, there is a grim determination about the way in which he set his feet towards the holy city. Or, put another way, a powerful sense of destiny, of fulfilling some divine plan, seemed to push him mile by mile along the hot and dusty roads that took him from the green fields of Galilee to the shimmering heat and rock-strewn hills of Judaea.

So it may have been with a sense almost of relief that on the Sunday before Passover, probably in the year AD 32, Jesus and his disciples crossed the last low line of hills between Bethphage and the valley of Kidron and made their way down the Mount of Olives towards Jerusalem. At last, they may have thought, the issue was about to be put to the test. Only Jerusalem, where the Sanhedrin – the priestly Council − sat, and where the great Temple enshrined the holy place and the Law of God, could pass judgment on a prophet. Only there could the Messiah be officially recognised.

As they came down the hillside, with Jesus riding on a borrowed ass, crowds of his supporters came out to meet him. As many had done before them to greet the arrival of a hero, they tore palm branches from the trees and laid them in his path – and some even threw their cloaks before him for the animal to tread on. And the shouts and singing would have echoed across the valley: 'Hosanna, Son of David – Save us now, Son of David!' It was a greeting fit for a messiah, yet with that touch of paradox that Jesus always seems to have assumed. The Deliverer, the 'Son of David', entered the city on an ass, rather than a noble charger. But in doing so, perhaps deliberately, he fulfilled a messianic prophecy of Zechariah: 'Behold, your King is coming to you, humble and mounted on an ass.'[1]

So the noisy crowd of his supporters would have wended their way into the city, probably through what was later called the Golden Gate. No doubt his entry created a stir. Many people in Jerusalem would have heard of the prophet Jesus from Nazareth in Galilee, but few would have seen him before – his visits to Jerusalem had been rather low-key affairs. But now, with the shouting, singing mob preceding him, it must have dawned on many people that the Galilean was, after all, a force to be reckoned with. He was, perhaps, rather more than just another hot-head from the North with a few rustic followers. It could well be that this noisy arrival in Jerusalem, more than any other single event, sealed the fate of Jesus.

For the next two or three days Jesus seems to have spent his time in and around the Temple – the magnificent 'Second' Temple, built by Herod, the site of which, even today, dominates the Old City of Jerusalem, and which at that time must have been a building of quite overwhelming grandeur.

His first gesture was ceremonially to 'cleanse' the Temple – again an almost self-consciously messianic act. Entering the courts where the sellers of pigeons and the money changers who provided the special Temple coins had their stalls, he made a scourge of ropes and drove them out, overturning their tables and crying, 'It is written, "My house shall be called a house of prayer"; but you have made it a den of robbers!'

The words he used are an interesting combination of a sentence from the book of Isaiah ('My house shall be called a house of prayer'[2]) and another from Jeremiah ('Has this house, which is called by my name, become a den of robbers in your eyes?'[3]). Undoubtedly Jesus saw himself in the same prophetic tradition. Jeremiah had spoken those words standing 'in the gate of the Lord's house' — the Temple — and had warned that if they were not heeded, and the Temple cleansed, then there would befall Jerusalem what had happened to Shiloh 'where God made his name to dwell at first' — it would be laid waste. Jeremiah's complaint about the religious practice of his time was very similar to that of Jesus: 'Will you steal, murder, commit adultery, swear falsely, burn incense to Ba'al and go after other gods that you have not known, and then come and stand before me in this house and say, "We are delivered!" — only to go on doing these abominations?'[4] It was the hypocrisy of an outward religion masking an inner impiety that appalled the prophets, and such hypocrisy is for Jesus the sin of sins. And here, in the very Temple of God, was the most flagrant and visible picture of it.

This 'cleansing of the Temple' by Jesus would have won him no friends in high places, for it was an attack on the heartland of the religious establishment. It was one thing to utter hot words up in Galilee; it was quite another to turn them into action in Jerusalem. Again, Jesus seems to have been sealing his fate by word and deed from the moment he crossed the Mount of Olives.

At any rate, the authorities could no longer ignore Jesus. He was not going to go away. So there followed a day or two during which the religious leaders subjected him to close scrutiny, sending scribes and elders to question him. The nature of their questioning betrays a certain hesitancy on their part. After all, they were mostly devout men, and they did not want to find themselves rejecting a prophet, or for that matter the Messiah.

So the questions centred on this: 'By what authority do

you do these things? And who is it that gave you that authority?' Of course the compilers of the Gospels, several decades later, inclined to ascribe bad motives to the religious leaders, assuming (not unreasonably, in view of later events) that they were simply seeking an excuse to destroy Jesus.

However, at this point in the sequence of events — and especially as we know that there was a division of opinion about Jesus even in the Sanhedrin itself — we may give them the benefit of the doubt and assume that they were genuinely trying to assess this unconventional 'prophet' from Nazareth.

In the event, Jesus's replies did not help them very much. He chose to answer either by asking another question about authority — 'Was the baptism of John from heaven or from men?' — or by relating parables, usually ones which spoke of the rejection of the truth by Israel and her subsequent judgment and even destruction. In both cases the thrust was the same: it was up to them to recognise the signs, to welcome the truth. Only disaster awaits those who reject the kingdom.

This was also the theme of a long discourse, variously reported by each of the first three Gospels, on the subject of the future — the 'little Apocalypse', as it is called. Piecing the different accounts together is difficult, but the general tenor of what Jesus was saying is fairly clear. The discourse seems to have been sparked off by an innocent remark by one of the disciples about the splendour of the Temple. Jesus said that the days would come when 'there shall not be left here one stone upon another that will not be thrown down' and then, when they asked when this would happen, and what 'signs' would precede it, proceeded to draw several graphic pictures of future calamity and disaster.

The difficulty in deciphering these sayings of Jesus is that it is almost impossible to decide whether he is speaking of one cataclysmic event — such as the destruction of the Temple in AD 70 — or of a number of events in the immediate and more distant future. For myself, I feel that this discourse presents two pictures. The first, and clearest, is of an immediately impending disaster which was to befall Jerusalem and the Temple. That was undoubtedly fulfilled in AD 70, when the Roman armies besieged the city and eventually destroyed it, virtually levelling the great Temple. We may leave the scholars to dispute how much, or how little, the original saying of Jesus has been coloured by the Gospel compilers, and whether they were writing before or after the cataclysmic event. I have no doubt at all that Mark's Gospel, at least, was written before AD 70 and that Jesus made some such prophecy. Both the language and the imagery have his own authentic style.

The second and more 'blurred' picture is of another great and cataclysmic event, further into the future. Here Jesus seems to have been developing the concept of the 'Day of the Lord', a crucial and final moment in history when God himself would call a halt to events and assume the mantle of power and judgment. The idea is found centuries earlier in the prophets of Israel, but Jesus gives it a new dimension.

The 'Day of the Lord', preceded by 'signs in sun and moon and stars', 'distress of nations' and 'the roaring of the sea and the waves', will have its climax in the coming of 'the Son of Man . . . in a cloud with power and great glory'.[5] In other words, Jesus puts himself in a central place in the coming Day of the Lord, which he sees perhaps as the final stage in the bringing in of the kingdom of heaven which he had preached.

I say that this second picture is 'blurred' because its images are archetypal rather than specific. With the earlier picture − of the destruction of the Temple − specific events are foretold, relating to known locations and clearly placed in the near future. But in the second picture the 'events' are more general: 'nation will rise against nation . . . men will faint with fear and foreboding for what is coming on the earth . . . there will be famines and pestilences in various places.' These dark images are the building blocks of the great picture of the Day of the Lord which has as its climax the return of the Son of Man.

The two pictures, as so often in prophetic writings, intermingle. It is hard for the present-day reader to know at times which one he is being invited to look at, and indeed it is possible that the prophet himself, Jesus in this instance, could not completely distinguish between the two. It is in the nature of a vision to offer images and symbols which the mind of the interpreter has to relate to people and events. And it is in the nature of apocalyptic writing – a recognised pictorial form of language at the time – to express truth symbolically, not literally.

What is certain is that here is no blueprint or timetable of future events, such as some have professed to discover. Jesus was not offering any such scheme or schedule, but a set of visionary pictures of the near and more distant future, to which he attached warnings about the dangers of resisting or rejecting God's will for his people.

It is true that some of the Christian churches of the first century – notably that at Thessalonika – seem to have taken these prophecies literally, but St Paul was at pains to warn them against any obsession with dates and timings.[6] Later, when they saw Jerusalem fall, as Jesus had foretold, they expected imminently the return of Jesus (the Son of Man) and the coming of the Day of the Lord. History has proved that they and others were wrong to expect an imminent fulfilment of the second prophecy, but in the nature of things 'history' cannot prove that it will not one day be fulfilled.

In any case, the 'picture' given by Jesus is not precise enough to enable anyone to construct a timetable from it. In its context, it is much more a kind of illustrated sermon, a vivid and dire warning that *in the end* God will triumph and the Messiah will be vindicated, whatever short-term setbacks may occur.

By the Wednesday or Thursday the religious authorities had had enough. Overcoming the objections of some of their Council, the chief priests and elders decided that Jesus must be arrested. With the Passover about to begin they felt the need to dispose of this troublesome Galilean before the feast, when vast crowds of Jews from other parts of the country, and from abroad, poured into Jerusalem. They were aware of the amount of popular support he had, and they had the added complication of the ever-watchful Roman authorities, so there was everything to be gained from a quick, quiet arrest, a brief, private trial and execution (if the Romans could be persuaded to agree to it) before nightfall on Friday, which was the day of Preparation before the Sabbath.

All the Gospels agree that Jesus was betrayed by one of the Twelve, Judas Iscariot, but the exact nature and extent of his betrayal is not clear. All that they specifically allege is that he agreed with the Jewish authorities to let them know when Jesus would be in a suitably quiet and private place where he could be inconspicuously arrested.

The chosen place was the garden of Gethsemane, at the foot of the Mount of Olives, where he had several times gone at night to pray alone, or with the Twelve. According to the Gospels, Judas identified Jesus to the waiting Temple guards by going up to him and kissing him, and they all allege that he was paid for this treachery — the notorious 'thirty pieces of silver'.

There is no doubt that the Gospel writers have given Judas a hard time. That is hardly surprising, given the circumstances. Once or twice we can catch them out, as they twist the knife in the wound.[7] No man who betrayed the Master was going to get sympathetic treatment.

This makes it all the more difficult to be absolutely sure of the facts about Judas. We may safely assume, so unanimous is the testimony, that he played some role in the arrest of Jesus, and that that role was interpreted as treachery by the others. It may well be that he did betray Jesus in exactly the way described, and even received money for doing so, without intending any harm to his Master. It may, as many have argued, have been a way of twisting Jesus's arm, of forcing him to reveal himself as the Messiah and Deliverer of Israel. It may also be that Judas simply wished to compel the Sanhedrin to consider the claims of Jesus formally, believing that if they did so they would recognise him as the Messiah.

What seems hard to believe (though not impossible) is that one of the Twelve, hand-picked by Jesus, should have been prepared to betray him for a comparatively paltry sum of money. Ambitious, money-loving men would never have followed Jesus in the first place, or would have given up after a few weeks of poverty on the road.

The betrayal (as we may call it) took place on the Thursday evening, after Jesus had eaten the Passover meal, the seder, with his disciples. At that meal, as we have already considered, Jesus instituted a ritual memorial of his own death, using the unleavened bread, the *matzos*, and the cup of wine which was drunk at the end of the meal as a thanksgiving. The bread, he said, was his 'body', broken for them; the wine was his 'blood of the covenant', which was to be poured out 'for many for the forgiveness of sins'.[8] It is doubtful if the disciples understood fully what he meant at the time, though they would certainly have seen the connection with the Passover, the sacrifice of the lamb, the use of its blood as a mark of deliverance,[9] and the institution of a new covenant between God and his people. But the event and the words clearly made a great impression, for we not only have them in more or less similar form in Matthew, Mark and Luke, but also in the considerably earlier first letter of Paul to the Corinthians. Paul spoke of the 'Lord's supper' as a rite based on a form of words which he had 'received': it was already deeply embedded in the life of the young Christian Church. When we compare his account with the accounts in the Gospels, we find a remarkable degree of similarity, indicating again how accurately the oral tradition could preserve a form of words.

'The Lord Jesus on the night when he was betrayed,' he wrote, 'took bread, and when he had given thanks, he broke it, and said, "This is my body which is given for you. Do this in remembrance of me."

'In the same way also he took the cup, after supper, saying, "This cup is the new covenant in my blood. Do this, as often as you drink it, in remembrance of me. For as often as you eat this bread and drink the cup, you proclaim the Lord's death until he comes." '

The meal during which this event occurred was, according to the synoptic Gospels, the Passover seder. John does not mention the bread and wine, but does describe a final meal which Jesus shared with the Twelve, at which he took the role of a servant and washed their feet. There is, in fact, a complication over dating between the first three Gospels and the fourth, because John has the crucifixion taking place on the first day of Unleavened Bread, when the passover lambs were sacrificed, whereas the others seem to place it on the next day, the Day of Preparation before the 'high' Sabbath of Passover. If John is right, then Jesus could not have eaten the seder meal with his disciples on the evening before his crucifixion.

In general, biblical scholars have backed the synoptic writers, and have argued that John was so anxious to associate the sacrifice of Jesus on the cross with the sacrifice of the Passover lamb that he allowed the symbolism to over-rule the facts. There have been many ingenious attempts at harmonising the accounts by scholars who wished to vindicate John's accuracy, but the difficulty remains.

However, it seems unlikely that the author of the fourth Gospel, writing with the earlier three Gospels in front of him, would have deliberately contradicted them over so specific a detail, especially when it is associated with so central a Christian doctrine as the crucifixion and resurrection of Jesus.

The director of the Jerusalem Centre for Biblical Studies, Yaacov Fleming, has a very persuasive explanation of the apparent contradiction. He set it out for me when I visited his centre over Passover 1981, but to the best of my knowledge he has not yet put it into print.

His theory is that the 'Last Supper' was celebrated in the guest chamber of an Essene community in Jerusalem. Fleming believes that a number of Essenes were among the followers of Jesus, and there is evidence of at least one Essene community resident in the city at that time. Indeed, the nearest gate to the traditional site of the 'upper room' is known as the 'Gate of the Essenes'. When Jesus was planning for the supper he sent two of his disciples to meet a *man* carrying a jar of water. Normally, the sight of anyone but a *woman* carrying a jar of water would have caused astonishment – perhaps, even, a riot! But if the man was an Essene, a celibate, a member of an all-male community, then he would have attracted little attention. Most people in Jerusalem would have seen Essene 'monks' carrying water.

This man was to lead the disciples to a large, upstairs 'guest chamber'. The Greek word *kataluma*[10] is not normally applied to a room in a home, but to a hall or chamber in an institution. It seems as likely as not that the 'Last Supper' did indeed take place in a *coenaculum* – guest chamber – in an Essene community in Jerusalem.

If that were so, then the explanation of the discrepancy between the dating of the Passover in the first three Gospels and the fourth Gospel may well lie in the Essenes' practice of celebrating Passover *one day before* the established date: such was their determination to separate themselves from the 'corrupt' Temple establishment.

In that case, Jesus and his disciples may have celebrated the seder meal on the Essenes' 'first day of unleavened bread', whereas the crucifixion would have taken place on the 'regular' first day, when, according to custom, the Passover lambs were killed between three p.m. and sunset – the time when Jesus was dying on the cross.

An alternative, though less colourful, explanation of the discrepancy is that, with Passover falling on a Sabbath that year, some may have chosen to celebrate the feast on the previous day, with the seder meal therefore on Thursday evening after nightfall.

Whatever day of the feast it was, however, there is little doubt that Jesus was arrested on Thursday evening, and that his various trials occurred during the night and early the next morning. It is again quite hard to construct from the Gospels a detailed order of events for these trials.

The general pattern of the accounts in the synoptic Gospels is clear, however. After his arrest, Jesus was taken to the high priest's palace for a preliminary interrogation, presumably to establish exactly what charges were to be laid against him. Then, at daybreak, the Council, the

Sanhedrin, met for a first 'hearing'. This would have been highly exceptional, with Passover already begun, and perhaps indicates how seriously the Jewish elders took the threat posed by Jesus to the establishment.

This hearing sought to establish charges of blasphemy against him, and once they were satisfied that he did not reject the title 'Son of God' (though he was careful not to claim the title himself) they felt the case was proven under Jewish law. However, they needed the endorsement of the Roman governor, Pilate, if Jesus was to be executed – and nothing less, they felt, would meet the needs of the case.

So Jesus was then taken to Pilate, where a completely different set of charges was proferred: 'We found this man perverting our nation, and forbidding us to give tribute to Caesar, and saying that he himself is Christ (Messiah), a king.'

It seems that Pilate was unwilling to get himself drawn into what he probably saw as a Jewish religious squabble. His reputation in secular history is of a particularly severe and brutal administrator, so the suggestions in the Gospels that he in some way supported Jesus, or strove to find a way to release him, can hardly reflect a troubled conscience. It is more likely that he saw the whole incident as yet another attempt by the Sanhedrin to usurp his authority and reinforce the theocracy that they believed Israel to be. It would then be in his interests to make things as difficult as he could for them and to ensure that any popular anger over the execution of Jesus would be directed at them, rather than him. In that, at least, he seems to have been successful.

According to Luke, Pilate tried to unload the case on to Herod, the tetrarch of Galilee, who happened to be in Jerusalem at the time, probably for Passover. But Jesus refused to answer Herod's questions, and he was then sent back to Pilate.

In a last attempt to foist the responsibility on to someone else, Pilate reminded the shouting crowd outside his palace that at the festival it was customary for him to release one prisoner of their choice, and he offered them Barabbas, or

Jesus. The crowd, possibly stirred up by the priestly party, shouted for Barabbas, who according to the Gospels had been sentenced for leading an insurrection in the city, and for murder. He was released; and Jesus – who declined to reject the title 'King of the Jews', though again he was careful not to use it himself – was taken away to be crucified.

The Barabbas incident is reported by all four Gospels, which is usually a good indication of historical authenticity. Probably at this stage of events, with Jesus remarkably passive in the face of impending execution, the crowd felt that a Zealot activist was of more value to their cause than a pacifist preacher.

So Jesus was put through the normal ritual preceding an execution. He was beaten, probably with the notorious leaded whip. He was ridiculed by the soldiers. His possessions – nothing more than the cloak he wore – were taken from him and shared among his executioners (though John reports that the soldiers cast lots for his coat, rather than tear it into pieces). Finally he was given his own cross to carry, and was led from Pilate's palace along the narrow streets of the city and out to a hill just beyond the wall, the place of execution.

Jesus had undoubtedly seen crucifixions. For a brief period in Roman history it was the normal method of public execution. It was at first confined to slaves, and to the end of its use, under Titus, it was regarded as the most shameful and degrading of all forms of execution. As the main objective was to deter other would-be offenders, the victims were usually hung on crosses at the roadside or at intersections, where they would be seen by the largest possible number of people. Jesus was crucified in a similarly public place, Golgotha,[11] the 'place of the skull', and there would no doubt have been hundreds if not thousands of onlookers.

It was also customary to put an 'accusation' over the prisoner's head, spelling out his crime for all to see. In the case of Jesus, the accusation was brief but ambiguous: 'Jesus of Nazareth King of the Jews'. It seems that the ambiguity was intentional – Pilate was determined to the last to remain neutral in any religious power-struggle amongst the Jews. The fourth Gospel reports that the chief priests complained about the wording of this accusation, preferring it to read, 'He said, I am King of the Jews', but that Pilate replied curtly, 'What I have written I have written'.

The death of Jesus is described in some detail in each Gospel, and it makes in all a sombre picture. They speak of two criminals who were crucified at the same time, and that certainly corresponds to the normal Roman practice. Undoubtedly there would have been the noisy wailing of the women mourning the deaths, and probably, as the Gospels describe, a good deal of shouting and jeering from the passers-by. With the city wall less than a hundred metres away, there would have been the noise and hubbub of the market, and the constant traffic of waggons, camels and donkeys. And there would have been the heat – by Passover time Jerusalem is very hot in the afternoon, and there would have been no shade from the sun out on Golgotha.

The Gospels record various brief sayings of Jesus on the cross: 'I thirst', 'My God, my God, why have you forsaken me?' and finally, 'It is finished'. Some, like the first of those, are simple requests for help. Some, like the second and third, plumb the depths of our knowledge of humanity and God. But none is more typical of Jesus, or more moving in its simplicity, or better attested as history, than the first words he uttered after they had nailed him to the cross and raised it into its position against the hot sky: 'Father, forgive them; they do not know what they are doing.'

He did not abandon that principle of acceptance, of forgiveness, which he had taught from Capernaum to Jericho, from Cana to Jerusalem, right to the very end. No words could have captured more precisely what it is about Jesus that sets him head and shoulders above his contemporaries, or what it is that makes him so irresistibly attractive to a race trapped in a cycle of blame and retribution. Even on the cross – *particularly* on the cross – he was setting people free from the consequences of their own folly and ignorance.

By late afternoon Jesus was dead. That is an important

point to establish, because there have been people from the earliest days (the Gnostics) right through history to the present day who have argued that he did not actually die on the cross.

Most of them suggest that he was deeply unconscious when he was taken down and put in the tomb, but revived, released himself (or was released by others) and rejoined his disciples. Thus, it is argued, the idea of a 'resurrection from the dead' gained credence.

However, it is an argument that does not bear serious examination. The Romans crucified thousand of criminals in the early decades of the first century — the practice was abandoned largely because of the colossal consumption of wood! There is no record of anyone surviving the experience. Medical experts have detailed the consequences of submitting the human body to crucifixion, and the injuries caused by the tearing and dislocation of organs and joints are demonstrably irreversible. It is true that it often took a long while for the victim to die, but it is totally inconceivable that a person who had been hung on a cross for six hours or more could possibly survive, let alone stand up or walk.

To hasten the end, it was established practice for the executioners to break the victim's legs, thus putting a sudden and fatal strain on the thorax. According to John's Gospel the soldiers came to break Jesus' legs, but found him already dead.

It is unlikely that they were mistaken. He had undergone the brutal scourging earlier in the day, and had been on the cross itself for six hours. Certainly, from all we know about the Romans and their executions, it is impossible to imagine that they would have refrained from breaking his legs if there had been the faintest possibility that he was still alive.

Before nightfall — the start of the Sabbath — his body was taken down from the cross. A wealthy supporter, Joseph of Arimathea, made his own private tomb available. It was near the place of crucifixion, in a garden. With so little time before the Sabbath, the body was simply wrapped in a shroud (if we are to follow the unanimous testimony of the synoptic Gospels), laid in the tomb — which was carved out of a rock-face — and shut in by a large, circular stone which was rolled across the entrance and sealed.

It was Friday night. The faithful women who had followed Jesus withdrew tearfully to mourn him. The other disciples, so far as we know, gathered disconsolately in a private room in the city, slowly adjusting themselves to the end of their hopes. The Sabbath came, the 'high' Sabbath of Passover, and the body of the man who had seemed, especially in those last few days, to cast himself in the role of a new Moses, bringing in a new Covenant for God's people, lay lifeless in a borrowed tomb outside the city wall.

# 11

# RESURRECTION

The death of Jesus, and his burial in a borrowed tomb, complete the historically verifiable story of his life. But if that were all there was to it, there is no reason at all why he should be remembered today. As we have seen, the contemporary records of his life are virtually nil, and if the crucifixion at Passover AD 32 (or thereabouts) had been the end it is extremely unlikely that he would have been considered important enough to have figured in the history books, beyond perhaps a marginal reference in specialist works on the period of the second Temple.

All that we know of Jesus, beyond those passing references in Josephus' history of the Jews, we know because very soon after the crucifixion his followers became convinced that he had risen from the dead. It is worth labouring the point, because it is frequently overlooked, both by his followers and their opponents. Almost everything that we know about Jesus was recorded by men who would never have written it down if they had not believed in his resurrection. That belief is a fact, as historically verifiable as anything we have touched on in this book. While in the nature of things, one cannot *prove* that Jesus rose from the dead, it is a matter of historical record that many of his contemporary followers believed he did, and were prepared to die for that belief.

The accounts of the resurrection in the Gospels are fascinating, and repay close study. They are not unanimous over details, but they are unanimous over the result. So far as the writers are concerned, two facts are beyond dispute: the tomb of Jesus was empty on the Sunday morning after the crucifixion; and Jesus was subsequently seen alive by many of the disciples.

The problem facing anyone who wants to establish precisely what happened is that the accounts in the New

Testament are quite extraordinarily difficult to synthesise. Whereas the first three Gospels usually tell more or less the same story, often in the same words, when it comes to the resurrection they seem to part company. And the fourth Gospel, as usual, has its own distinctive record of events. Over some details the Gospels appear to contradict each other (how *was* the body of Jesus prepared for burial?) and it is virtually impossible to harmonise the various accounts of the discovery of the empty tomb on Sunday morning. Some scholars have even claimed that Luke contradicts himself, as between his two accounts of what has become known as the 'ascension' of Jesus[1] — though this seems a rather far-fetched allegation.

If we start with what seems clear and certain, we can be pretty sure that Jesus was buried in a tomb belonging to Joseph of Arimathea, a member of the Jewish Council, near the place of his crucifixion.

That in itself is an important detail to establish. It was not normal practice for the bodies of criminals executed by the Romans to be buried privately. Usually they were buried ignominiously in common criminal graves within an hour or two of their execution. In view of the public interest in and support for Jesus, one would have expected the authorities to insist that the normal procedure should be carried out in his case.

However, if the Gospels are right in identifying Joseph of Arimathea as a member of the Council, then it begins to make sense that the 'usual procedure' was not followed. It seems likely that at that point in time Joseph was a sympathiser, but not yet a disciple. We know that another member of the Council, Nicodemus, was also a 'sympathiser' — and there may well have been others.

In other words, there had been all along a faction on the Jewish Council which supported Jesus, or at any rate was unhappy about moves to arrest or execute him. As the chief priest's party had had their way over the execution, they may well have felt it to be diplomatic to appease the pro-Jesus party over the comparatively unimportant detail of the burial. Certainly without that support in high places there is no doubt that the body of Jesus would have ended up in an anonymous criminal's grave outside Jerusalem.

The second thing that seems clear and certain is that the tomb was empty on Sunday morning. This is common to all the Gospels, and though it is not mentioned it is certainly implied in the earliest account we have of the resurrection, by St Paul.[2] In the Gospels, various men and women visited the tomb on Sunday morning, and all found it empty, though they did not automatically deduce from that that Jesus had 'risen'.

The third certain thing is that the disciples were publicly preaching that Jesus had risen from the dead by the feast of Pentecost, seven weeks later, and that from that point the 'Church' – the body of believers – grew rapidly in Jerusalem and, when persecution began, far beyond.

The fourth certain thing, as we have noted earlier, is that the leading disciples − the so-called 'apostles' or 'special messengers' − were convinced that Jesus had appeared to them alive during a period of six weeks or so after the crucifixion. They had 'seen the Lord'. They stuck to this belief in the teeth of ferocious opposition, persecution and even, for many of them, execution. That does not prove that what they believed was historical fact, of course, but it does seem to prove that they were not fabricating the story, or parties to some kind of a conspiracy. People do not die for such things.

Of these four elements in the resurrection 'event', the two that have evoked the greatest controversy and scholarly scepticism, especially in recent years, have been the 'empty tomb' and the 'appearances' of Jesus to the disciples. Many modern writers have suggested that the idea that Jesus was in some way 'alive' took root among his followers in the period after his death and later gave rise to the stories of the empty tomb and the various appearances of Jesus which are related in the Gospels. In other words, what they call the 'Easter faith' *preceded* the accounts of the 'Easter event', and the whole resurrection is to be explained as an interior experience by the disciples later externalised in the stories we have in the Gospels.

In fact, as a number of distinguished theologians have pointed out in recent books,[3] this theory simply does not explain the known facts. It appeals to people who want to remove all traces of the supernatural or transcendent from religion, but it will not satisfy those who are more concerned to establish what actually *happened*, on the basis of evidence.

As we have seen, followers of Jesus were preaching that he had 'risen' — that he was alive again — seven weeks or so after the crucifixion, in the very city where it had taken place. It seems inconceivable that they could have done so, or would have been believed, if the body of Jesus was at that very moment reposing in a nearby grave. It would not have been difficult for the authorities to exhume it and silence the apostles once and for all. That they did not do so suggests either that they could not, or did not want to. We know beyond any doubt that they wanted to stifle the 'Jesus movement', which was seen as divisive and blasphemous, so presumably they could not produce the body, and the only rational reason why they could not is that it was not there.

Over the centuries many theories have been put forward to account for the absence of the body. Some have suggested it had been stolen by tomb-robbers, others that the disciples went to the wrong grave, others that the disciples themselves removed the body and hid it. Frankly, none of them stands up to serious examination. The events surrounding the execution of Jesus were public — sufficiently public to enter into the historical records of the Jewish nation. It is inconceivable that the authorities would not have taken steps to guard the grave (as Matthew reports[4]) and ensure that this notorious trouble-maker caused no further trouble. Tomb-robbers of the first century were not interested in cadavers, which were of no commercial value whatever, but in the jewellery, linen and other effects that were in the tomb. Yet the Gospels record, in passing, that the linen wrappings were found in the tomb on the Sunday morning. If that is fact — and it is the sort of detail that has the ring of truth — then we may rule out tomb-robbers as the removers of the body.

One must also, I think, rule out the disciples. It is hard to see what motive they would have had for removing the body beyond deliberate and pre-meditated deception. But all their subsequent behaviour, the pattern of their lives, the sincerity of their speeches and writings, and their willingness to die for the truth of the resurrection, suggests that they were genuinely convinced of the resurrection, and were not remotely the kind of people to hatch out and carry through such a bare-faced plot.

I suppose it is just possible that the disciples went to the wrong grave on the Sunday morning. But when they started proclaiming that Jesus had risen from the dead, it is surely beyond belief that the authorities would make the same mistake. It is more than likely that every possible tomb in the area was ransacked in search of the body . . . but if so it was never found.

However much the idea of the 'empty tomb' was developed by the Church long after the event, it rests on a pretty convincing historical base. As John Coventry, the Master of St. Edmund's House, Cambridge, has written: 'It is in the highest degree improbable that anyone at the time would have believed the proclamation of the first witnesses that Jesus had risen and appeared to them, if in fact this had not been coupled with clear evidence of an empty tomb.'[5]

The fact is, of course, that many people 'believed the proclamation', for the rapid growth of the Christian Church in the first few decades of its existence is a matter of historical record. *And it all turns on the resurrection.*

As St Paul wrote to the Church at Corinth, about twenty years later, 'If Christ has not been raised, your faith is futile.' It was this belief that galvanised and motivated the first believers and it was on this faith that the Church was built − a Church which both the Roman and Jewish authorities sought desperately to destroy. It was in their interests to disprove the resurrection, for that was the obvious way to cut the roots of the Church's very existence. It was in their interests; they had the resources and will to do it: but they did not. Indeed, so far as one can tell, they made no serious attempt to do it. Their failure is, in its way, the most convincing historical evidence for the resurrection of Jesus. It may be difficult to believe that the tomb was empty on the Sunday morning; but it is almost impossible to believe that the body of Jesus was in it. That is not a statement of religious faith, but a sober assessment of the evidence of history.

The empty tomb was not, however, the predominant element in the first preaching of the resurrection. When the disciples, some seven weeks after the event, started to assert to the Jewish crowds in Jerusalem that Jesus, the Messiah, had risen from the dead, the key argument was one simple statement: 'We have seen the Lord.'[6] It was the evidence of their own eyes to which they appealed: 'We can all bear witness.'[7]

In Paul's summary of the gospel message to the Corinthians, he uses the same verb, in the passive voice, three times: '[The risen Jesus] was *seen* by Cephas, then the twelve, then he was *seen* by James, then by all the apostles: last of all he was *seen* by me.' Again there have been attempts at arguing that these appearances were simply interior 'experiences' of Jesus − that the disciples became aware by some rebirth of faith that the man they had followed from Galilee to Jerusalem was still 'alive', in some sense of the word. From this experience, they came to speak of him as having 'appeared' to them, been 'seen' by them in an interior spiritual vision.

But − attractive as this theory may be to some modern scholars − it is impossible to find it in the New Testament. The disciples may have been deluded, but the language they use to describe their experience simply cannot be forced to convey this kind of sophisticated interpretation. When they say 'I have seen the Lord' or (in the passive voice) 'Jesus was seen by Cephas' they are − to quote John Coventry − using the 'simplest of Greek words and commonest of Greek constructions'. How, he asks, 'could the Corinthians be expected to understand some such refined meaning as "God made known interiorly" from such straight-forward language?'

He goes on: 'The evidence seems irresistible that "I have seen", quite independently of scene-setting stories, is where it all started. And it conveys something equivalent to objective seeing, and not an interior conviction.'[8]

If we are to understand the New Testament as its original writers intended, we must avoid reading into it twentieth-century ideas and conditioning. No one can really argue that the apostles did not believe that they had seen the risen Jesus – the 'Lord', as they now preferred to call him. And it seems unlikely that the frightened, depressed and defeated little band who hid themselves in Jerusalem behind locked doors 'for fear of the Jews' could have become the bold apostles of the resurrection unless something totally convincing and irrefutable had happened to them. They say they saw the Lord. It takes a rash person two thousand years later to argue that they did not.

The record of those appearances of the risen Jesus, however, raises some problems. In Matthew, the appearances (after Sunday morning) are all in Galilee. In Luke, they are all in and around Jerusalem. In John, they are in Jerusalem and Galilee. It is difficult to harmonise the details, or to work out any kind of a time-scale – phrases like 'some time later' or 'after many days' seem to conflict with other accounts that suggest the whole sequence of appearances occurred within a single day.

However, it is possible to make too much of these difficulties. In one sense, they are powerful arguments for the authenticity of the reports, because they completely exclude any element of collusion between the witnesses. They all tell the same basic story – that the disciples, to their astonishment and joy, 'saw' the risen Jesus in a series of appearances; that at first some had doubts or were sceptical of the reports of the resurrection (especially, and typically, the reports of 'the women'[9]); and that eventually the appearances came to an end after the apostles had been commissioned by Jesus to carry the good news to the world at large.

It is not at all surprising, within that framework, to find a variety of incidents and locations. Indeed, it is consistent with an event which was both shocking and unexpected that accounts of it are somewhat garbled and unclear.

For myself, I should suspect a tidy, waterproof account of the resurrection. That would smack of propaganda. What we have, in fact, is a series of sketches, of reminiscences, of impressions of events that burnt themselves into the memories of those who were involved.

Undoubtedly Matthew, Luke and John each preserve a different set of resurrection stories, each representing a different oral tradition. The church in Jerusalem undoubtedly preserved one such set of accounts, which is perhaps the basis of Luke's narrative. But there was also a church in Galilee, and Matthew may have had access to their stories. John may well represent a source descending directly from the apostolic eleven — certainly he has a number of convincing details of human reactions and group dynamics which suggest the evidence of an eye-witness.

In any case, taken together the accounts of the appearances of Jesus represent a formidable body of evidence that something happened to the disciples which changed their dejection and disillusionment at the crucifixion into a powerful and convincing belief in the resurrection. I do not see how this can be attributed simply to some experience, some 'second wind of confidence' on the part of the eleven.

That is, as John Coventry argues,

'flat against the evidence. All the evidence points to complete dejection and loss of hope among the disciples: there is no evidence at all for a rallying of faith and courage coming from inside of them. No: the evidence is that something happened *to* the first witnesses, which was of a sudden and totally unexpected nature, and not a product of their own rallying enthusiasm.[10]

So the disciples believed, as Christians believe today, that Jesus 'rose' from the dead. Clearly the body of Jesus that they saw after the resurrection was different from the one he had had before. This 'resurrection' body was not confined by time, space or matter. It could move through locked doors and across considerable distances. It had, it seems, a changed appearance: time and again those who knew Jesus well failed to recognise his risen form — Mary of Magdala, Cleopas and his companion on the road to Emmaus, Peter, Thomas, James and John at Tiberias — only to realise it was 'the Lord' through some uniquely typical word, gesture or action. It was the way he said 'Mary', the way he broke bread and said the thanksgiving, the way he worked his 'miracles', that convinced them that this was the self-same Jesus they had known and loved and followed.

And he was not a ghost or apparition, of that they were quite clear. Obviously the risen body of Jesus was in some sense a spiritual rather than material body — after all, as St Paul says, 'flesh and blood cannot inherit the Kingdom of God'.[11] But it was the body of Jesus – a man they had known so well – and not a mere apparition of it that they saw. Christians believe, of course, that this was the 'resurrection body' that in due course all will share – the new vehicle for human personality, fitted for life in the spiritual realm with God for ever.

The accounts of the resurrection all agree that these appearances came to an end, but only Luke rounds them off with a description of the 'ascension', when Jesus finally took leave of his disciples and disappeared from their sight in a cloud.[12] There are hints of the same event in Matthew[13] but none at all in the fourth Gospel. Presumably on each of his 'appearances' Jesus eventually 'disappeared', so perhaps the distinguishing mark of his final appearance was what he said — his 'last words'. There seems little doubt that they were a final act of commissioning, and that what we see in the history of the early Church is that commissioning being fulfilled by the apostles.

The events of Pentecost, when they were 'filled with the Holy Spirit' in a vivid, mystical experience, seem to have been the seal on that commissioning, the proof that Jesus meant what he had said when he promised to be 'with them' and 'in them', 'even to the end of the age'.

It is never easy to record profound spiritual experiences, and it is even harder to interpret and assess them long after the event. Obviously what the Gospel writers describe as occurring after the crucifixion falls into the category of a 'profound spiritual experience', and it is not surprising that people have differed in their interpretation and assessment of it. But the central fact is clear, and it is the thing that makes Jesus different from other prophets and religious founders, and Christianity different from other religions. Jesus was crucified, died and was buried. But, from the third day after, those who knew him best were convinced that he was alive, that his tomb was empty, and that they had 'seen the Lord'.

# 12

# JESUS, 'CHRIST' AND 'LORD'

About forty years ago a group of archaeologists unearthed from the sands of Egypt a scrap of papyrus, bearing a couple of dozen Greek words. Upon examination, it was found to be a fragment of St John's Gospel, part of the conversation between Pontius Pilate and Jesus at his trial. The experts were also able to date it — it was written about AD 130. That tiny bit of parchment is the earliest manuscript we have of any part of the New Testament, and its discovery caused some scholarly embarrassment, because a number of distinguished New Testament scholars of earlier times, like Baur and Pfleiderer, had confidently argued that the fourth Gospel had not been written by that date.

In fact, what has happened over recent years is that the fourth Gospel, the one we know as 'St John', has been re-established as an historical document, after over a century of scepticism. So much so that recently one of Britain's leading New Testament scholars, John Robinson, has argued that it is as early as the other Gospels, being written before AD 70, and may be regarded as the historical framework into which the others have to be fitted.[1]

In my own reconstruction of the 'Jesus of history' in the earlier chapters of this book I have not drawn very heavily on John's Gospel. It still seems to me that in establishing the message of Jesus and the main events of his life the synoptic Gospels, depending upon the oral traditions of the Church and perhaps written sources like 'Q', are the basic tools. But now, having attempted that reconstruction, and turning to the most important question of all, 'What is the *meaning* of Jesus?', the time has come to take up the fourth Gospel, and see what it has to tell us. It will carry all the more weight for its new-found (or freshly re-discovered) historical authority. But its main value to us has always been its brilliant insight into the person and meaning of Jesus.

It is called 'John's' Gospel, and nowadays almost all scholars agree that it was written by John — but *not*, in most cases, the Apostle John. From the earliest years of the Church until 1792, when an English critic, Edward Evanson, raised doubts about it, the authorship of John the Apostle was unquestioned. After all, the book is claimed to be the work of an eye-witness;[2] this witness is called 'the disciple whom Jesus loved', who is generally identified as John;[3] and the author is obviously very well versed in the geography of Israel, and probably his mother-tongue was Aramaic.

But other considerations raised doubts. If the book were the direct work of one of the Twelve, would he have used parts of Mark and Luke, as John appears to have done? Would John the Apostle have styled himself 'the disciple whom Jesus loved'? And would there be so enormous a difference in style, phrasing and even content between the Jesus of the fourth and the Jesus of the other Gospels if an apostle were its author?

The argument is in fact finely balanced, because very early witnesses, like Irenaeus, writing in AD 177 and quoting Polycarp, who was born in AD 70 and was a disciple of John, claim that the Gospel was the work of the apostle.

The general consensus of scholars today is that the book shows so intimate a knowledge of the Holy Land, has so many evidences of eye-witness knowledge and has so clear an air of authority about it, that if St John did not write it himself, then whoever did write it was a close associate of his. As William Temple puts it: 'I regard as self-condemned any theory of authorship which fails to find a very close connexion between the Gospel and the son of Zebedee [the apostle John]'.[4]

Many modern scholars believe that it was actually written by another John, 'John the Elder', as they call him, who was a devoted disciple of the Apostle John. A fourth-century document names as bishops of Ephesus 'Timothy ordained by Paul and John ordained by John' — and tradition almost universally locates the origin of the Gospel at

Ephesus. A.M. Hunter summarises the position like this: 'If we are to put a name on the title page of the fourth Gospel, there is no better candidate in the field than John the Elder, and we may neatly describe the Fourth Gospel as "The Gospel of John (the Elder) according to John (the son of Zebedee)".'[5]

The authorship question is important, because the value of the Gospel lies in its intimate and authoritative assessment of Jesus, rather than in its detailed narrative of events, and that assessment would be somewhat devalued if it were the work of a writer in the second century who never met Jesus and had no special or personal knowledge of him or his mission. The likelihood that it records, or echoes, the words and thoughts of John the apostle, one of the closest associates of Jesus, obviously greatly enhances the value of this book.

The fourth Gospel *is* different from the others, almost certainly intentionally so. It did not set out to provide yet another account of the birth, baptism, teaching, miracles, death and resurrection of Jesus (though most of them are present in John's account), but to tell the Church what they meant. And if it is the work of an apostle, or based on the recollections and assessment of an apostle – especially one as close to Jesus as John clearly was – then we may be as sure as it is possible to be that we are getting the true meaning – the 'meaning' Jesus himself gave – to his life and work.

Before we start to consider that 'meaning', however, we should look at the matter of the alleged difference between the Jesus of the first three and the Jesus of the fourth Gospel. That there is a difference cannot be denied. The 'synoptic' Jesus talks like a rabbi. He deals in homely stories and robust moral sayings. His language and his illustrations alike are earthy, direct and uncomplicated. The Jesus of John's Gospel, on the other hand, uses no parables or stories, and seldom sounds like a rabbi. His language is profound, abstract, almost philosophical, though it is true that such illustrations as he uses are drawn from the ordinary life of farm and village. There is, quite simply, nothing in the first three Gospels from the lips of

Jesus that is even remotely like 'I am the resurrection and the life' or 'Unless a man is born again he cannot see the kingdom of God', or 'I and the Father are one'. Nor is there anything in John's Gospel from the lips of Jesus that sounds remotely like 'The sabbath was made for man, not man for the sabbath', or 'Give to the one who asks you, and do not turn away from the one who wants to borrow from you', or 'I have not come to call the righteous, but sinners'.

Some people have pointed out that John's favourite phrase on the lips of Jesus is 'eternal life', while the synoptics speak of 'the kingdom of God'. And, of course, one can list the incidents which John omits: the baptism (though it may be inferred), the transfiguration, Gethsemane, and the Last Supper. Or the incidents which he includes and the others omit: the conversations with Nicodemus and the woman at the well; the raising of Lazarus; the water into wine at Cana; 'doubting Thomas' and the resurrection appearance by the Lake Tiberias.

Yet it is too simple by far to conclude from this some contradiction between John and the other Gospel writers. After all, John had almost certainly read Mark and Luke, and he would have been as aware as we are that his Gospel was different in important ways. Whatever he did was not accidental, nor was it done in ignorance of the synoptic accounts. To take one instance, the synoptic phrase 'the kingdom of heaven (or of God)' is in fact paralleled by the phrase in John 'eternal life', rather than contradicted by it. They look and sound different, but their meaning is almost identical. Indeed, it is quite an interesting experiment to interchange them and see how little difference it makes to the sense of a passage. The 'kingdom of heaven' was Jesus: it became present in him. 'Eternal life' is Jesus: 'in him was life.'

We can also discount the theory that John wrote his Gospel to correct the others, or even to contradict them. There was no such controversy in the early Church, nor any hint that its leaders felt John corrected or contradicted the other Gospels. Indeed, the Christian writers of the second and third centuries would boast of the sound four-legged base on which the Church was built. The four Gospels, taken together, were seen as complementary, not contradictory.

Again, the leaders of the early Church were not simpletons. They, like us, could read, and they too must have been aware that the chronology of John — the order of events — was different, that in his Gospel Jesus spent much more time in Jerusalem, and that his Jesus, as we have seen, speaks differently from the Jesus of the synoptics. Yet they seemed to find no problem in it.

The reason, I am sure, is in the perspectives of the different Gospels. Those early Christian leaders knew, because it was a common-place in the writings of the early Church, that John was not setting out to write an account of the life of Jesus. They had that already, three times over. He was trying to give them, on the basis of intimate and personal knowledge, an understanding of that life.

The difference can be seen in the opening of the Gospels. Luke and Matthew start with the birth of Jesus. Mark begins with his baptism. But John begins in heaven: 'In the beginning was the Word, and the Word was with God . . .' For John the story of the life of Jesus did not begin at Bethlehem or the Jordan, but in heaven, where the Word — the expression of God's will — shared in creation and the giving of life and light to mankind. That Word was now to become 'flesh': 'and the Word was made flesh, and lived among us'.[6] So Matthew, Mark and Luke, in their own different ways, tell us what happened. John, in his own way, tells us why.

I think this also accounts for the difference in the speeches of Jesus recorded in the first three Gospels and the amazing discourses set out in the Fourth.

Perhaps an analogy may help. If we wanted to know what Winston Churchill said in a particular speech in 1942, we could look up the contemporary newspaper records. There we would find, perhaps, a few sentences, taken down in shorthand by a reporter, with possibly a summary of the main arguments of his speech. We would have some of his actual words, but we might well feel that the flavour, meaning and significance of the event eluded us.

But supposing we had access to one of his closest friends and colleagues, who was present when the speech was given – who had, perhaps, discussed it with him in advance, and argued with him about it afterwards. He might not remember a single sentence verbatim, but there is little doubt that he could convey, even forty years later, the impact and meaning and significance of the speech far better than the newspaper accounts of it. Similarly, I believe that the synoptics are closer to the actual words of Jesus; John, however, may well convey to us *more accurately* what they meant.

It is worth remembering that there are no quotation marks in New Testament Greek, so it is often impossible to tell where the writer is intending to quote verbatim, where he is summarising the original speech, or where he is giving his own comments or amplification of it. This is especially true of the fourth Gospel; but if the 'reporter' is a person who knew the speaker well, understood his ideas and is honestly attempting to convey them – as we may be sure John is – then the loss of the verbatim speech is not at all serious.

Of course, John's Gospel, like the others, is a product of the post-resurrection Church. It is shot through with the writer's faith that the person he is describing and whose ideas he is trying to represent is in fact the risen Lord. None of the Gospels is a straight, factual, neutral, contemporary account, but John's, more than the others, is clearly the child of long reflection on the meaning of Jesus. So, time and again, he will admit that at the time of the event the disciples did not see its significance, but that later, after the resurrection, they could interpret it correctly.[7]

So this fourth Gospel gives the Christian today, or the modern 'enquirer', the priceless benefit of an interpretation or assessment of the meaning of Jesus from someone ideally qualified to do it, after the event (of course), but not so long after as to make distortion inevitable. This is Jesus as he seemed to one of his closest friends as he looked back at his life – not less than thirty years after the event, or more than sixty. This is how someone almost uniquely well placed to do so assessed the life of Jesus of Nazareth, whom he had come to believe was the Messiah ('Christ', in Greek) and then, probably later, 'Lord'.

We know, from the synoptic Gospels, that the disciples took a long while – perhaps a year, possibly two – coming to the belief that Jesus was the Messiah.

We also know that even after the resurrection they were not sure about the nature of his mission. According to Luke, they were still asking whether he was about to 're-store the kingdom to Israel'[8] – a nationalistic political view of his mission which Jesus had explicitly rejected in their hearing many times. But John, looking back on the events, sees Jesus from first to last as 'the Lord'. He was recognised as the Messiah by several of the disciples at the time of their calling. Everything he did — his 'signs', as John calls the seven miracles he relates — is confirmation to them that Jesus is the Messiah, and also the 'glorious' Son of God. So, at the end of the story of the water into wine, John comments: 'This, the first of his signs, Jesus did at Cana in Galilee, and manifested his glory; and his disciples believed in him.'[9]

This is a fascinating example of the difference between the first three and the fourth Gospel. Mark, Matthew and Luke record the observable fact that the disciples did not confess Jesus as the Messiah until they were in Caesarea Philippi, at the start of the last stage of his ministry. John recollects the evidence on which that confession was based, and recalls, undoubtedly truthfully, that at each stage, from the first day that they met Jesus, the disciples responded to that evidence. Faith is not, usually, something that comes in an instant, as a kind of 'package' to be received. It grows, step by step, in response to evidences and experiences. So the disciples could ask Jesus, 'Lord, increase our faith'.[10] So Jesus could compare their faith to a tiny mustard seed, at the moment small and vulnerable, but capable of growing into a strong and sturdy tree.[11] Faith is not a static thing, and as we look back at our lives and try to see how we came to the beliefs and commitments that we now hold, we see things differently. We are, often, more charitable about our earlier doubts and hesitations, seeing them as steps towards a full and assured faith. John sees the faith of the disciples through that long perspective. Jesus was, from the first, immensely impressive. Every word, every action, spoke of a man who was more than merely human. That is what John now sees, with the eye of experience: 'The word became flesh and dwelt among us, full of grace and truth; we have beheld his glory, glory as of the only Son from the Father.'[12]

So let us now try to see the Jesus John gives us, remembering that he is not the Jesus the crowds would have seen in Galilee or Jerusalem, or the Jesus of historical reporting, but Jesus as those who knew him best, *and believed in him*, came to understand him. We have seen the 'Jesus of history'. This is the 'Jesus of faith'.

We have already noted the fact that John does not start his Gospel at Bethlehem, where Jesus was born, or at the Jordan, where he began his public work, but in heaven, where, as the eternal 'Word', he shared the glory of the Father. For John, the over-riding truth about Jesus, which illuminated every incident and every word spoken in his life, was that he is the 'only Son of the Father'. The life of Jesus simply did not begin at Bethlehem. Indeed, it never 'began', because he shared the Father's nature from eternity: 'He was with God in the beginning.' He was even the agent of creation itself: 'Through him all things were made; without him nothing was made that has been made.' And he is the very source of life itself: 'In him was life, and that life was the light of men . . . The true light that gives light to every man was coming into the world.'[13]

According to John, this divine 'Word', the agent of creation, 'the only Son, who is at the Father's side',[14] was now about to enter human history: 'The Word became flesh and lived for a while among us'.[15] And that staggering event − the coming of 'God's only Son' into the world of space and time − happened at the birth of Jesus. 'For a while' the source and origin of life itself walked the paths of Galilee and pushed his way through the crowded, noisy markets of Jerusalem.

But why had he come? John's answer is different from (though not, I believe, contradictory to) the one given by the synoptic Gospels. They describe Jesus in the setting of the Israel of his day, pointing to a different solution to the nation's ills, offering a new way of love and acceptance instead of hatred and revenge. For them, he is the 'prophet, Jesus of Nazareth', who acts and talks like the Messiah, and who is eventually accepted as that by his followers. And, of course, that belief is confirmed by God raising him from the dead.

John, however, looks back at the life and work of Jesus — through the perspective of faith — and sees something more. The synoptic Gospels record the 'miracles' of Jesus. John records similar stories, but for him they are 'signs' — they 'signify' something. The choice of a different word epitomises a different motive in reporting them. Matthew, Mark and Luke all record the incident of the feeding of the five thousand. For them it is amazing, memorable, a convincing demonstration of the power of Jesus. John tells the same story, but for him it is a 'sign', and it leads straight into a long explanatory discourse about the 'Bread of Life': 'The bread of God is he who comes down from heaven and gives life to the world.'[16] The whole miracle is about Jesus the life-giver. For him, the 'miracles' are always symbols of deeper truth. They illustrate who Jesus is, and what he came to do. John believes Jesus is the Messiah, of course. But he goes much further. The Messiah is not simply God's messenger or agent, like a latter-day Moses or Elijah. He is, in some mysterious way, God himself.

So John records discourses of Jesus in which the relationship of the Father and the Son is worked out. Undoubtedly these have their sources in conversations which Jesus had with the disciples — or perhaps, more specifically, with the inner core of the Twelve, Peter, James and John. It may well be that some of them are also based on things that Jesus said publicly, though they are conspicuously absent from the first three Gospels. It must also be, however, that they are the product of John's own reflection on what he heard and saw, and his interpretation of it in the light of the resurrection, the giving of the Holy Spirit at Pentecost, and the life of the growing Church.

In these discourses two things emerge. The first is that Jesus is subject to the Father: 'the Father is greater than I'.[17] All through his life, obedience to the Father's will was the determining factor for him. However much John wanted to stress the divinity of Jesus, he was nevertheless in no doubt that the Ruler of the Universe and the supreme Authority of the 'Godhead' was the Father.

The second element in this relationship was to be held in tension with that: the Father and the Son shared the same nature. 'I and the Father are one.'[18] For John, Jesus is, quite simply, divine: 'What God was, the Word was.'[19] So the most appropriate title for him, and the one that became normative after the resurrection, was 'Lord': 'God has made this Jesus, whom you crucified, both Lord and Christ.'[20]

For John, then, the Jesus of history is the Lord of glory,

'the divine Christ who came forth from the bosom of the Father, unveiled him to men, died for the world's sin, rose again and passed to the right hand of God, whence he comes again through his Spirit to those who love him. In short, he shows us Jesus not as a figure of ancient history but as the eternal contemporary, the light of the world, the only true and living way, now as then, to God.[21]

It is necessary to ask ourselves at this point whether such a belief is valid. Was John so devoted to Jesus — or to the memory of Jesus, which is not quite the same thing – that his view of him is hopelessly extravagant? When we put the Jesus of the fourth Gospel – 'the only Son from the Father's side' – alongside the Jesus of the first three Gospels – 'Jesus of Nazareth' — are we not driven to conclude that John has detached himself completely from any historical base and is simply describing some inner vision of an incarnate deity?

I do not think we are. In fact, I think the evidence drives us the other way, to the conclusion that John's Gospel is a commentary on or explanation of the others, showing us the meaning of the 'Jesus of history', and that without it the accounts given us by Matthew, Mark and Luke are seriously inadequate.

For instance, the discourses in John, as we have seen, explore the relationship between the Son and the Father. It might be thought that there is nothing of this kind in the synoptic Gospels, but in fact, and typically, there is, in a brief and embryonic form: the single word *Abba*. The Aramaic word quoted by Mark almost certainly underlies other places where Jesus spoke of God as 'Father'. It is a term of intimacy used (so far as can be told) by no one else of God. As A.M. Hunter puts it:

> What research shows is that *Abba* was the name Jewish children used in addressing their human fathers; but no God-fearing Jew would have dared to apply it to the holy God. The first to do this was Jesus and, in default of other evidence, this word alone would testify to the uniqueness of his filial communion with God.[22]

John, of course, was also a God-fearing Jew. From his mother's knee he would have been indoctrinated with the idea of the 'one God' – the fundamental difference between Judaism and all the other religions of the ancient world. Any notion of a plurality of gods was sheer blasphemy, a pagan corruption of the purity of the religion revealed to Israel through its patriarchs: 'The Lord our God the Lord is *One*.'

If we are right in assuming that John the son of Zebedee is the primary source of this Gospel, or that it is the product of someone who was his disciple and shared this thinking, then the fourth gospel is a record of Jesus by someone who knew him well. It is impossible to live with someone for nearly three years, day in and day out, in triumph and adversity, and not get to know them pretty well. We may safely assume that few people, if any, knew Jesus of Nazareth – that is, the 'historical' Jesus – better than John did.

Yet here we have a man – a God-fearing Jew – whose

deeply-rooted conviction is that God is 'One', actually arguing that his best friend, a man whom he knew intimately and had watched in all the everyday occurrences of life, is divine, shares the nature of God, is 'God's only Son'. Why on earth should a devout Jew come to that conclusion, unless it were inescapable?

The title 'Lord' reinforces the argument. We have become so used to calling Jesus 'the Lord' or 'our Lord' that it has no element of shock or scandal for us. It is simply a title, like 'Sir' or 'the Reverend', with little specific meaning.

But for the first Christians it was a word of immense significance, so that to call Jesus 'Lord' was regarded as the single, conclusive proof of Christian faith. Indeed, so awesome was it, so unimaginable in human terms, that the name could only be applied to him by those who were spiritually endowed to do it: 'No one can say "Jesus is Lord" except by the Holy Spirit'.[23]

St Paul quotes in his letter to Philippi an older Christian hymn. By the nature of things this must date from the early years of the Christian Church. And here, in this 'primitive' hymn, is the same notion of the awesome power of 'the name that is above every name' — and the 'name', given by God to Jesus, is 'the Lord'.

Therefore God exalted him to the highest place
And gave him the name that is above every name,
That at the name of Jesus every knee should bow,
In heaven, and on earth, and under the earth,
And every tongue confess that Jesus Christ is Lord,
To the glory of God the Father.[24]

The word translated 'Lord' is *Kurios*, and to give some idea of its meaning for a devout Jew one can simply say that Matthew's Gospel uses it in its opening chapter as a name of God, Jehovah: 'All this took place to fulfil what the Lord (*Kurios*) had said through the prophet'. Indeed, the Septuagint (Greek) version of the Old Testament uses *Kurios* to translate 'Lord' when referring to Jehovah. It is true that it is also used in New Testament Greek as a mark of respect, the equivalent of 'sir', and also for a sovereign or potentate. But when it is used as it is in the Philippian hymn, the whole context demands a title of quite extraordinary dignity and power, and *Kurios*, the word chosen, has that association with God and his authority and majesty which does indeed bestow an extraordinary status upon Jesus.

Clearly this was exactly what Paul and the other apostles intended. Their understanding of Jesus was that he is 'Lord', and that the resurrection established his right to that title. Peter argued this on the day of Pentecost, using one of the most popular Old Testament verses in the early Church: 'The Lord [God] said to my Lord [Jesus], sit at my right hand until I make your enemies a footstool for your feet.'[25]

'The Lord' is the normal New Testament title for Jesus after the resurrection, but for Paul and John, particularly, it is a title that expresses not what he *became* but what he is and always has been. The disciples had not always understood it, even those who knew Jesus best. But the resurrection, and the gift of the Holy Spirit which followed it, 'opened their eyes'. They began to see that all that Jesus had said and done, every miracle or 'sign', every sermon or story, every detail in his suffering, crucifixion and resurrection, pointed to the same conclusion: Jesus is the *Lord*.

At this point of history they were not laying down complicated theological formularies designed to express this revelation in a permanent, credal statement. They were perhaps even unaware of some of the questions that later generations were to raise about the precise nature of the divinity of Jesus, and his relationship to the Father. They were, I believe, simply giving expression to the universal experience of the Church. Jesus of Nazareth was the Messiah, so they called him 'Christ'. And he was the 'only Son of the Father', so they called him Lord.

Now the people who did this were not later generations of believers who, looking back, invested the historical Jesus with an aura of the supernatural. It would be understandable if his later followers, separated from the man Jesus by several decades, vast distances, and a cultural chasm, had endowed their founder with god-like power and dignity. It has happened in history, it happened in the Graeco-Roman world, and it may happen again.

But the evidence is that the title 'Lord' was first used of Jesus by the apostles themselves, the very men who had lived and worked with him and knew him best. He was not, for them, some rather remote, shadowy figure from the past, the eponymous founder of their religion, a being whose natural place would be at the right hand of God in the majesty of heaven. Far from it. He was Jesus, the son of Mary, the carpenter, the rabbi, their companion and friend.

They were Jews. They guarded the names and dignities of God with meticulous reverence. They did not lightly accept a man as the Messiah; and by every normal assessment, they would never call any human being 'the Lord'.

But they gave that title to Jesus — not long after the event, but immediately. They knew he was human. They came to believe, as John Coventry puts it, that he was also 'somehow to be identified with the being of God himself'.[26] If we can begin to imagine what it must have taken to bring them to that belief, then we can also begin to see the weight of the evidence that Jesus was no 'ordinary' man, nor even an 'ordinary' prophet. For them, calling Jesus 'Lord' was a kind of spiritual Rubicon. Once it was crossed, there was no going back. But they crossed it, and they were prepared to die for their belief that Jesus of Nazareth was the Messiah, 'Christ', and the Son of God, 'the Lord'.

# 13

# THE MEANING OF THE CROSS

To the casual reader it probably seems strange that by far the greatest emphasis of all four Gospels is on the death of Jesus. In proportion to its duration, the last week of the life of Jesus is given a quite extraordinary prominence – roughly a third of the Gospels is taken up with those seven days. The two to three years of the ministry of Jesus, or the thirty years of his life in the case of Matthew and Luke, are compressed into the other two-thirds. The inescapable conclusion is that for the first followers of Jesus his death (and resurrection) were of absolutely paramount importance.

We have seen already how the resurrection – or, more precisely, the disciples' experience of the risen Lord – transformed a dispirited rabble into an evangelising force. It was the resurrection, and the subsequent experience of being 'baptised by the Holy Spirit', that gave birth to the Church, and it is obviously true to say that if Jesus had remained in the tomb Christianity would never have been born. It is the child of the resurrection.

But it is also true that very soon after the resurrection the disciples saw that the crucifixion of Jesus, too, was central to his mission. It was not just a cruel and unjust end to a noble life, nor simply a necessary prelude to the resurrection (what has not died cannot be raised), but in a vivid way it epitomised everything that Jesus was and all that he set out to do.

According to John, the last recorded words of Jesus were the cry, 'It is finished'.[1] In fact, it was one word in Greek, *tetélestai*, and it carries the sense not simply of something being over but of something being accomplished. When a candle has burnt out it is 'finished', and when a craftsman completes the last touch on a table it is 'finished'. The word used by John conveys the second rather than the first sense

— a task, a mission had been accomplished. It is not a cry of defeat, but of satisfaction. So the early Church came to see the cross not as an object of scorn or shame, or as the sign of defeat or despair, but as the culmination of the entire mission of Jesus. 'The Son of man did not come to be served, but to serve, and to *give his life* as a ransom for many.'[2]

This idea of Jesus 'giving' his life for others, or even as a 'sacrifice', is a central theme of many passages in the letters of Paul.[3] It is explicit in John's Gospel.[4] And, as we have seen, it is even to be found in the synoptic Gospels. So wide is the testimony to it, and so integral to the earliest records of Jesus, that it seems to me irresistible that we are here touching on a fundamental belief of the first Christians. Baptism itself, the basic rite of initiation into the Church, was identified from the earliest years with the death of Jesus: 'Don't you know that all of us who were baptised into Christ Jesus were baptised into his death?'[5] It was no coincidence to the early Church that Jesus died at the Passover. He was the passover Lamb, offered up in order to deliver God's people from slavery and evil.

So we find all through the letters of Paul the phrases 'for me' or 'for us'. Christ died 'for me'. He offered himself as a sacrifice 'for us'. He is 'our passover'. He did not die pointlessly or fruitlessly, nor did he die for his own sins. He had not committed any. He died for sins, it is true, but they were *our* sins: 'Look, the Lamb of God, who takes away the sin of the world!'[6]

Now some people have argued that this whole idea of the death of Jesus as a sacrifice for sin was the invention of the post-apostolic Church. For them, the simple story of Jesus of Nazareth, who came on his mission to the people of Israel and was crucified, is all that we have. The resurrection was an inner experience of faith, not an observable fact. The divinity of Jesus was the result of a Jesus-cult, strongly influenced by various movements and ideas common in the Graeco-Roman world. And the idea of the 'atonement' – the sacrifice of Jesus for the sins of the world – was a predictable development of the divinity and resurrection beliefs: obviously a 'God' cannot be killed. He can only lay down his life voluntarily.

Again, however, the evidence seems to be against this. The notion that Jesus died 'for' us, as a sacrifice for sin, is as strong in the earliest letters of Paul as in the later ones: perhaps stronger. Indeed, it occurs in that earliest of all creeds, in the letter to Corinth: 'Christ died for our sins.' It is in the accounts of the institution of the eucharist ('this is my body, given for you . . . My blood poured out for many for the forgiveness of sins') which are undoubtedly primitive, and it was thus celebrated or commemorated from the very birth of the Church. It is in the baptismal formulae, as we have seen. It is a thread running through the fourth Gospel. It seems to me beyond doubt that the apostles themselves believed it, at least from the time of the resurrection onwards.

However, did *Jesus* believe it? Did he believe, as he was being crucified, that he was the new Passover Lamb, being offered up as a sacrifice for sin? Or was this an interpretation put on the event by the apostles, after the resurrection, to tally with their new belief in him as the Lord from heaven?

In one sense, of course, we can never know, because we do not have any independent contemporary records of what Jesus said and taught. We have to rely on the testimony of those who had come to believe in him as Lord and Messiah. However, no one suggests that they were not right in their unanimous testimony that Jesus went up to Jerusalem at the Passover, and was crucified then. Few would deny that the Gospels are accurate in reflecting a feeling of inevitability about the death of Jesus, or that he himself expected to be put to death in Jerusalem. And most scholars regard the words of institution at the Last Supper as authentic, at any rate in their briefest form.

Given those considerations, we may safely assume that Jesus deliberately went up to Jerusalem at the Passover expecting to be arrested and executed; that he chose the time at least partly because of its symbolic significance; and that he regarded his death in some way as an offering of himself which would inaugurate a new 'covenant' or agreement between God and his people.

From there it is a minor step to accept that various statements attributed to Jesus in the Gospels referring to his death amplify this intention. We have already quoted Matthew's reference to his death as a 'ransom', a price paid to free slaves. Mark has the identical wording. John's Gospel, of course, has many explicit statements about the death of Jesus. Like a grain of wheat, he must die in order to produce a good harvest.[7] Just as Moses once lifted up a brass snake on a pole, to heal those who had been bitten by a plague of snakes, so the Son of man must be 'lifted up' so 'that everyone who believes in him may have eternal life'.[8]

The statements in the fourth Gospel may well not be the words of Jesus himself, but John's own interpretation of them. However, they undoubtedly reflect John's understanding of the intentions of Jesus, and, even allowing for the influence of hindsight, suggest that the disciples were aware that he saw his death as special, significant and even fore-ordained.

The first Christians connected the death of Jesus with a new way of forgiveness. Mark and Luke both record that at the moment of the death of Jesus the 'veil of the Temple', which curtained off the Holy Place, was torn in two from the top to the bottom. Whatever else this strange incident implies, it clearly symbolised for them a new access to God, and one that was meant to replace the complicated system of animal sacrifices which had obtained since the time of Moses. So it is not surprising that Paul and Peter, in their letters, see the death of Jesus as a sacrifice for sin. It is one of the great themes of Paul's letter to the Romans: 'What the law was powerless to do in that it was weakened by sinful nature, God did by sending his own Son in the likeness of sinful man to be a sin offering'.[9]

Over the centuries of Christian history millions of words have been written about the precise meaning of the death of Jesus. Theory has vied with theory. Was his death an expiation or propitiation for sin, a price demanded by a holy God for the forgiveness of a sinful human race? Was it 'substitutionary' – a death 'instead of' the sinner, or 'in his place'? Was it a sin-offering, like that made by Jews under the old dispensation? All these, and many more, have been argued on the basis of the New Testament texts and their Old Testament counterparts, and one can certainly find hints, and more, of all of them in the Bible.

However, if we confine ourselves – as we are trying to do – to the core of the message of Jesus in the New Testament, then many of these complications dissolve. Jesus saw himself as the Messiah, having a unique relationship to the Father, and with a unique 'mission'. Part of that 'mission' was to proclaim the 'kingdom of God'. Part of it was to demonstrate or confirm the presence of the kingdom by healings and exorcisms. Part of it was to establish a whole new way of looking at truth. And part of it was to die 'for' mankind, as the 'Suffering Servant' prophesied by Isaiah.[10]

That, in brief, seems to have been how Jesus saw his own mission. His friends and followers were slow to see the full implications of it. They responded initially to the idea of the 'kingdom'. The moved on to the belief that he was the Messiah. They began to share his new perspective on truth. They accepted his 'special relationship' to God. And, reluctantly at first, but with mounting conviction after the resurrection, they came to believe that his death was the key to everything else about him. Far from being the defeat they had previously thought it to be, the end of their hopes for the deliverance of Israel,[11] they saw it as the perfect demonstration of the kind of love he had talked about. It was the full vindication of his claim that evil could be overcome with good. It would bring in the 'kingdom'. And it was proof that forgiveness and acceptance are part of the very nature of God – or why did God raise him from the dead?

During the following decades the Church struggled to put these ideas into a dogmatic form. Nearly twenty centuries later it has still not succeeded in doing so. While the great 'catholic' creeds are explicit about the person and nature of Jesus, about the Holy Spirit and the resurrection, they confine themselves to the barest of statements about the cross: 'He was crucified for us under Pontius Pilate, died, and was buried'.

Yet the cross remains the most powerful symbol in the history of mankind. It is entirely fitting that so cosmic a symbol cannot be confined within verbal formulae. The cross is what life is like in the common experience of our race. Evil flourishes, the innocent suffer, good appears to be defeated, death always has the final word. And God, if he exists at all, seems remote from his struggling, suffering creatures.

But the cross also shows us the reverse of that picture. Evil is first absorbed and then defeated. Innocence is vindicated. Good triumphs. And death, as Paul triumphantly cries, 'has been swallowed up in victory'.[12] Far from being a symbol of despair, the cross has become for millions of people an instrument of hope. It actually *creates* hope. Or, rather, what Jesus did in facing evil head on, allowing it to break his body and shed his blood, creates hope. It tells us that God is not by any means remote from his struggling, suffering creatures, but in the body of his Son struggled and suffered . . . and overcame.

This understanding of the cross, of course, can only come to those who believe that the person who died on it shares the divine nature; and that he rose from the dead. If he were merely a creature like ourselves, his death would simply take its place in the long list of travesties of justice that marks the history of the human race: sad, regrettable, appalling, but in no way unique. And if he had remained dead, then evil would have triumphed, and death would have had its customary last word.

So it is not surprising that belief in the death of Jesus as a sacrifice for sin — as the sign of a decisive change in the relationship between God and mankind – *followed* belief in him as Messiah and Lord, and in the resurrection. It is, in a sense, a logical development from those beliefs, for if Jesus were indeed the Son of God then his death must have had meaning, and certainly the purpose of God could not be thwarted by a handful of Jewish ecclesiastics.

The difficulty for a modern reader, I think, is to see the

connection which the New Testament assumes between the change in the relationship between God and mankind, on the one hand, and this notion of a 'sacrifice for sins', on the other. In our world-view, based very largely on dynamic relationships, we can see that a great gesture of love and acceptance can break through a situation and utterly transform it. Modern people, on the whole, have little difficulty in seeing the cross of Jesus in that way. God's Son seized the initiative in the endless struggle between good and evil, and the antipathy that it creates between God and his rebellious creatures, and in one magnificent moment of self-offering showed us that whatever else God is — holiness, purity, justice – he is also, and supremely, love. That we can, for the most part, understand.

But sacrifice, in the ritual sense, is literally beyond us. Unlike the ancient world, we have no concept of appeasing the righteous anger of God by offering him a sacrifice. Indeed, we tend to think of the very idea as barbaric. So the concept of Jesus offering himself as a sacrifice, to pay the penalty due for the world's sin, is also incongruous and even distasteful to modern people. We cannot see why God needed it, and we cannot see what it achieved.

But while sacrifice in a ritual sense seems remote from us, its underlying concept is surely common to all human experience. We, like our forefathers, can understand a mother 'sacrificing' her life to save her child, or a man 'sacrificing' his career for love, or even a politician 'sacrificing' his principles, as we say, 'on the altar of expediency'. In every case there is a common motif: a price has to be paid. Nothing, as we often tell each other, is for nothing. Anything worth having costs something. There is a price to be paid for every advance in human understanding, every worthwhile relationship, every change for the better. We would be as suspicious as they were in the ancient world of anyone who told us that there could be gain without pain.

So, without complicating the issue with the notion of blood sacrifices and ritual offerings which were so central to the Old Testament religion, we can nevertheless enter into the idea of the costly sacrifice that achieves great ends. We may find the idea of Jesus being offered up on the altar of the cross as a sacrifice for sin[13] difficult and incongruous, but that does not mean that we cannot understand that sin and evil are serious distortions in the universe, and that defeating them requires that a great price should be paid. Christians have traditionally spoken of the 'blood of Christ' as that price: 'You were redeemed . . . with the precious blood of Christ, a lamb without blemish or defect'.[14]

At heart, the cross of Jesus tells me something of what it cost to deal with the problem of sin in the world, in human nature and in me. It excludes the possibility of 'cheap grace'. It gives the phrase 'the love of God' meaning and reality, because it demonstrates what his love for his creatures cost his Son. Jesus died a real death for real sin: the cross was no empty charade. In that sense, no modern person ought to reject the idea of the 'sacrifice' of Jesus. A price had to be paid, and he paid it: 'Greater love has no one than this, that one lay down his life for his friends. You are my friends . . .'[15]

# 14

## THE SEARCH FOR JESUS

I begun this book by saying that I wanted to help the 'ordinary' believer to 'correct his vision of Jesus', and the interested unbeliever to be faced by Jesus as he is. Researching it has had a remarkable impact on my own faith. Rather like a restorer of old pictures, I was constantly amazed and delighted as the layers of old varnish came off and a fresh, vital image emerged – the one, I hope, that the original artist intended. I also hope that something of that experience has been shared by both groups of readers.

I have talked of the 'Jesus of history' and the 'Jesus of faith'. There was a man who lived, preached, healed and died in Palestine just under two thousand years ago. The fact that Christians since his death have come to regard him as the Messiah and the Son of God cannot obscure his existence as a person of history. We are not free to lay upon that person views he did not hold, claims he did not make, or an aura he did not have. At different times in history people have wanted him to play different roles – as a divine Visitor from 'the other world', perhaps, or as an ethereal Lover or a revolutionary Leader. But we are shut in to the Jesus who existed: Jesus of Nazareth. Like it or not, he is the founder of Christianity, and as a religion rooted in history it cannot re-draw its Founder's beliefs and characteristics to suit the need of the moment.

The Jesus of history is an attractive person, and few who study his life closely come away from the exercise unchanged. Many are driven to the conclusion, as I am, that the disciples were entirely right to claim that he was more than a prophet, more, even, than the Messiah. They called him 'the Son of God' or 'God's only Son', and by that word 'only' they meant that he was not just 'a son of God' – many had been given that title, and in a sense we are all 'sons' and 'daughters' of God – but had a unique relationship with the

Father: indeed, that he shared his essential nature.

But it is the 'Jesus of faith' with whom we are concerned today. Of course it is important to understand as accurately as we can what Jesus of Nazareth was like, what he said and did, and how he died. But an accurate grasp of that information does not make a Christian. A Christian is someone who has shared with the apostles that 'Easter experience', who, like them, has met the risen Lord and received the gift of the Holy Spirit. There is, of course, a direct connection between the Jesus of history and the experience of the risen Lord, but our knowledge of the former is only valuable (in ultimate terms) if it leads us to the latter. Christianity is not a study course in antiquities.

We can see the process in the early Church, from a few days after the resurrection. 'Jesus' quite quickly becomes 'the Lord'. Very soon 'Christ', which was at first a description of his role ('Messiah') has become a title and then a name. St Paul, certainly, uses it as a synonym for Jesus or the Lord, occasionally putting all three together in one long title: the Lord Jesus Christ.

The first Christians were overwhelmed by Easter. The resurrection obviously took them by surprise, and it must have been difficult for them to relate the Jesus many of them had known 'in the flesh' to the glorified 'Lord' who was the object of the Church's worship. However, it was easier for them, I think, than for their successors, and it is hardly surprising that history has seen great swings of attitude towards Jesus. Sometimes he has been so 'divine' as to be barely recognisable as a man at all. Sometimes, especially in recent decades, he has become so 'human' that it is hard to imagine how any of his contemporaries could ever have regarded him as 'the only Son of the Father'. Today, probably most unbelievers favour the 'human' Jesus, rejecting the claims for his divinity. Many believers, on the other hand, still cling to quite extravagant ideas about his nature on earth, arguing that he knew everything that God knows – including, say, quantum mechanics and the details of future history – and that he knew them even in his cradle.

The difficulty is not a new one. It is to hold in balance two complementary truths about Jesus. He was a human being, limited as we all are by the restrictions of time, space and our own brains and bodies; and he was uniquely related to God, open to him in a way we are not, sharing his divine nature. We cannot make Jesus so 'human' that he is not truly divine, nor so 'divine' that he is not truly human.

For me, the answer is to concentrate on the Jesus of the Gospels – all four of them. The picture they present has an intrinsic balance, so that we can see him whole. Indeed, for me, the man they portray must be the Son of God, and the Son of God they portray must be a man.

I have said that 'Easter' overwhelmed the first Christians. The danger today is that that Easter experience may be missing from our Christianity. Probably hundreds of thousands of people saw and heard Jesus during his life. Some questioned him closely. Some followed him, attracted by his message. But only a handful, comparatively speaking, met the risen Lord, and they were the ones who founded the Church and turned the world upside down. Christianity is a religion of resurrection, but it is more than that: it is a religion of the personal experience of the resurrection. To this one and that one, in and around Jerusalem and in Galilee, the risen Jesus appeared. After that experience, there was no more doubting: 'We have seen the Lord'.

It may seem unfair to end a book which is mainly about historical evidence by introducing the subject of personal experience, especially to claim it as the determining feature in Christian faith. But it would be dishonest to do otherwise. Believing 'correctly' about the Jesus of history does not make me a Christian; meeting the risen Lord *does*.

I do not mean, of course, that Jesus is still 'appearing' to people. As we have seen, those appearances ceased a short while after the resurrection. What I do mean is that the search for the Jesus of history only makes sense if it leads on to the Jesus of faith – the Lord Christ – and that faith in him *is* a matter of experience. It is not a blind leap, because we base it on our understanding of the Jesus of history. But it is a response to an initiative by God, just as those first Easter experiences were. If we seek Jesus, and want to put our faith in him, he will come to us, just as surely as he came to Mary of Magdala, Thomas, Peter and the others: not in a vision, but in the kind of inner conviction that has fired every real believer from that day to this.

I should like to address my last words to that 'interested unbeliever'. How can an interest in Jesus, or even respect or admiration for him, turn into that kind of faith? How can the search for the truth about him, on which we have been engaged, turn into that 'seeking' for him that he promised he would reward?[1]

I believe that the Jesus of faith is to be found in two places. One of them we have been searching closely – the New Testament; and this may well be the moment for the reader himself to pick up the Gospels again, and read them through, like biographies, preferably in only two or three sittings. The Acts of the Apostles and St Paul's letters could follow. In this way it is possible to recapture both the reality of Jesus and the way those first Christians responded to him.

The second place of search we have hardly considered. It is the Church. In this strange, ill-defined, massive association of human beings, Jesus promised to be present: 'Where two or three of you meet together in my name, I am there among you.[2] He founded it, at least embryonically, and it has ever since claimed to be the guardian of the truth about him and the fellowship of those who believe in him.

Of course the Church has failed Jesus, and often fallen woefully short of the ideals and truths for which he lived and died. Of course it has at times been corrupt, at times ineffective, and at times it has looked and behaved like the worst kind of worldly tyranny. Yet even in its darkest days the light of Jesus has also shone there. Men and women of faith and holiness have carried on that mission of love and acceptance.

It is very easy to dismiss the Church as an institution, or to say rather glibly that we admire Jesus but despise the body he founded. Yet it is a fact that every day of every week men and women are coming to faith in him *within the Church*. It is still the place where he meets the perplexed, the doubting and the seeker. And, with all its faults, it still 'represents' him in the world.

May I make a specific suggestion to anyone who finds it hard to imagine how one can come to the experience of faith? It is simply to go to a communion service in a church. For the sake of the experiment it does not matter which denomination, or whether they call it the Lord's Supper or the eucharist or the mass. Slip in and sit at the back, watch and listen. This ritual goes back in an unbroken line to that evening when Jesus shared the 'seder', the Passover meal, with his friends. Those taking part are sharing in something that has been done millions of times over through nearly twenty centuries, in obedience to the words of Jesus: 'Do this, in memory of me'.

As the service goes on, and the bread is broken and the wine poured out, it is possible to begin to feel in a new way how trivial a thing time is. What is being done is all, in essence, so simple, yet it is also almost unbearably profound. In one symbolic moment the Jesus of history, who broke the bread and gave thanks, and the Jesus of faith, who still meets his people, are united. The priest faces the congregation and says, 'The Lord is here', and it becomes possible to believe that it is so.

The New Testament shows us Jesus as he was, and as he became to the first believers. The Church shows us Jesus as he is, and as he has become to believers today. At the eucharist, more than at any other moment, they seem to be one and the same. It may well be that the search for Jesus of Nazareth, which starts at Bethlehem or by the Jordan, and leads by way of the cross to an empty tomb, ends where bread is broken and wine is shared. It would be fitting for him to meet us there, for on that first Easter evening at Emmaus, sitting down to a late supper with two bewildered and discouraged disciples, Jesus took the bread, said the blessing and broke it. At that moment, Luke tells us, 'their eyes were opened and they recognised him'.[3] Their discouragement and tiredness forgotten, they set off on the

seven miles back to Jerusalem to find the other disciples.
'Then they told,' he records, 'what had happened on the
road, and how Jesus was known to them in the breaking of
the bread.'

In that moment, for them, the Jesus of history and the
Jesus of faith met. So, in our different age, in our alien
culture, but in that same simple action, we also may find the
real Jesus. We shall discover, as they did, that it is too
simple to say that the real Jesus is the man from Nazareth,
not the risen Lord of the early Church. Rather, like them,
the more clearly we see and understand the real Jesus who
walked the lanes of Galilee, the easier it will be to believe
that he is also the one who 'ascended far above all things',
the 'real' Lord Christ at whose name the whole creation
bows. There *is* only one Jesus, not two; and the search for
him ends when the two pictures of him − so often and so
unhelpfully set against each other − come together, as they
did for the disciples at Emmaus and as they do every time
Christians today 'do this' in memory of him.

# BIBLIOGRAPHY

Coventry, John, *Faith in Jesus Christ*, Darton, Longman and Todd.

Dodd, C.H., *The Founder of Christianity*, Collins.

Edwards, David, *Jesus for Modern Man*, Fontana.

Ferguson, John, *Jesus in the Tide of Time*, Routledge and Kegan Paul.

France, R.T. and Wenham, David, *Gospel Perspectives* (Vols. 1 and 2), JSOT Press.

Grollenberg, Lucas, *Jesus*, SCM.

Hunter, A.M., *Introducing New Testament Theology*, SCM.

Hunter, A.M., *Introducing the New Testament*, SCM.

Mackey, James P., *Jesus, the Man and the Myth*, SCM.

Marshall, I. Howard, *I Believe in the Historical Jesus*, Hodder and Stoughton.

O'Collins, Gerald, *The Easter Jesus*, Darton, Longman and Todd.

Ramsay, A.M., *Jesus and the Living Past*, Oxford University Press.

Riches, John, *Jesus and the Transformation of Judaism*, Darton, Longman and Todd.

Robinson, John, *Can We Trust the New Testament?*, Mowbray.

# NOTES

## 1: THE JESUS OF HISTORY

1   by John Robinson.
2   edited by John Hick.
3   by Don Cupitt.
4   by E. Schillebeeckx.
5   *Read, Mark, Learn*, Fount.
6   In a BBC radio broadcast, May 29th, 1977.

## 2: WHAT IS THE EVIDENCE?

1   In a BBC radio broadcast, May 29th, 1977.
2   *Jesus, the Man and the Myth*, SCM.
3   Ibid., p. 124.
4   Ibid, p. 157.
5   1 Cor. 15: 3–7 (J.B. Phillips).
6   That is, those written by AD 70, or thereabouts.

## 3: THE FIRST RECORD: MARK

1   1 Tim. 3:16.
2   1 Cor. 15: 3–5.
3   Rainer Riesner has demonstrated how important memorization was in the life of the Jews of the time [*Gospel Perspectives* (Vol. 1), JSOT Press]
4   Mark 11: 20, 21. Cf. Matt. 21: 18, 19, 20.
5   In the early second century, Papias described Mark as 'the interpreter of Peter'.

## 4: THE GOSPELS AS EVIDENCE

1   Col. 4:14.
2   *Introducing the New Testament*, SCM, 1957.
3   E.g. Acts 16:10 ff.
4   Acts 21:8.

5   Luke 2:2 – see Chapter 6.
6   Matt. 2:23.
7   Luke 2:51.

## 5: JESUS COMES TO JORDAN

1   Luke 3:8.
2   Luke 1:36
3   Matt. 3:14 certainly suggests this.
4   See, e.g. Luke 21:35.
5   Mark 6:3.
6   Mark 8: 27–30.
7   See, e.g. Mark 8:30, Matt. 17:9.
8   John 12:29.

## 6: THE BIRTH OF JESUS

1   John 8:41.
2   Mark 6:3.
3   For an interesting attempt to harmonise history and midrash in this passage, see an article by R.T. France in *Gospel Perspectives* (Vol. 2), JSOT Press.
4   Luke 2:48, 49 (J.B. Phillips).

## 7: WHAT WAS THE 'MESSAGE' OF JESUS?

1   Luke 11:20.
2   Luke 17:21.
3   John Riches, *Jesus and the Transformation of Judaism*, Darton, Longman and Todd, pp. 107–9.
4   Matt. 3:8.
5   Matt. 5: 44, 45.
6   Luke 7:9.
7   Matt. 23:24.
8   Luke 13:31 and Matt. 22:23 ff.
9   E.g. Luke 14: 1–6.
10   Mark 2:23 and 7:2.
11   Mark 2:27.
12   E.g. Mark 2:16.
13   Mark 2:17.

14   Matt. 5:39, 5, 9.
15   John 18:36.
16   Matt. 7:7, 8.
17   Matt. 7:28, 29.
18   *Who Was Jesus?* BBC.
19   See, e.g. *Son of Man*, by Maurice Casey, SPCK.
20   Dan. 7:13, 14.
21   *Jesus, the Man and the Myth*, SCM.

## 8: WHAT JESUS DID

1   Luke 11:29.
2   *Jesus in the Tide of Time*, Routledge and Kegan Paul
3   Luke 13:16.
4   John 9:2, 3.
5   Luke 4:18–19.
6   Luke 19:5
7   Luke 14:21.
8   Matt. 15:1, 2.
9   Luke 7:33, 34.
10   Jer. 31:31–4.

## 9: WHAT WAS JESUS LIKE?

1   Isa. 53:2.
2   Luke 15:11 ff.
3   Luke 16:1–9.
4   *The Original Jesus*, by Otto Borchert, Pickering and Inglis.
5   Matt. 23:24, Luke 7:25, John 4:17, 18.
6   Luke 13:33, 34.
7   *The Original Jesus*, p. 181.
8   Mark 10:37.
9   Luke 9:54.
10   I.e. Matthew, Simon the Zealot and Peter.
11   John 4:4 ff.
12   Luke 10:38–42.
13   Matt. 15:21–28.
14   Luke 8:43.
15   Lev. 15:19

16   Luke 6:20.
17   Luke 18:24, 25.
18   Luke 12:16 ff.
19   Luke 16:19 ff.
20   John 3:17.
21   Mark 1:40–42 and Luke 5:12–14.
22   Mark 12:37.
23   John 21:25.

## 10: THE LAST WEEK

1   Zech. 9:9.
2   Isa. 56:7.
3   Jer. 7:11.
4   Jer. 7:9, 10.
5   Luke 21:25 ff.
6   1 Thess. 5:1, 2.
7   See and compare Matt. 26:8 with John 12:4–6.
8   Matthew 26:26–28.
9   See Exod. 12:13.
10   The Latin equivalent is *coenaculum*, a guest chamber.
11   In Latin 'Calvary'.

## 11: RESURRECTION

1   Cf. Luke 24:50–3 and Acts 1:6–11.
2   1 Cor. 15: 3–7.
3   E.g. Raymond Brown, *The Virginal Conception and Bodily Resurrection of Jesus* (Geoffrey Chapman) and John Coventry, *Faith in Jesus Christ* (Darton, Longman and Todd).
4   Matt. 27:65, 66.
5   *Faith in Jesus Christ.*
6   See, e.g. John 20:18, 20:25 and 1 Cor. 15:5–8.
7   Acts 2:32.
8   *Faith in Jesus Christ.*
9   Luke 24:10, 11.
10   *Faith in Jesus Christ.*
11   1 Cor. 15:50.

12   Luke 24:50, 51 and Acts 1:1–11.
13   Matt. 28:16–20.

## 12: JESUS, 'CHRIST' AND 'LORD'

1   In *Re-dating the New Testament* (SCM) and subsequent papers.
2   John 1:14.
3   John 13:23, 19:26, 20:2 ff, 21:7, 20.
4   In *Readings from St John's Gospel*.
5   In *Introducing the New Testament* (SCM).
6   John 1:14.
7   See, e.g. John 2:22.
8   Acts 1:6
9   John 2:11.
10   Luke 17:5.
11   Mark 4:31, 32, Matthew 17:20.
12   John 1:14.
13   John 1:2–9.
14   John 1:18.
15   John 1:14.
16   John 6:33.
17   John 14:28.
18   John 10:30.
19   John 1:1 (NEB).
20   Acts 2:36.
21   A.M. Hunter, *Introducing the New Testament.*
22   *Introducing New Testament Theology* (SCM).
23   1 Cor. 12:3.
24   Phil. 2:9–11.
25   Acts 2:34, 35. (The words in brackets are, of course, mine.)
26   *Faith in Jesus Christ.*

## 13: THE MEANING OF THE CROSS

1   John 19:30.
2   Matt. 20:28.
3   E.g. Rom. 5:8.
4   E.g. John 3:16, 6:51.

5   Rom. 6:3, 4.
6   John 1:29.
7   John 12:24.
8   John 3:14, 15.
9   Rom. 8:3, 1 Pet. 2:24.
10   Isa. 53.
11   Luke 24:21.
12   1 Cor. 15:54.
13   Heb. 13:10.
14   1 Pet. 1:18, 19.
15   John 15:13, 14.

## 14: THE SEARCH FOR JESUS

1   Matt. 7:7.
2   Matt. 18:20.
3   Luke 24:31.